World Tour

ACKNOWLEDGEMENTS

Editorial and Design by Tall Tree Ltd

Illustrators: Mike Love, Pippa Curnick, David Shephard, Michelle Todd, Cherie Zamazing
Publisher: Piers Pickard
Art Director: Andy Mansfield
Editorial Director: Joe Fullman
Editor: Christina Webb
Print Production: Nigel Longuet

Published in July 2021 by Lonely Planet Global Ltd

CRN: 554153
ISBN: 978 1 83869 457 9
www.lonelyplanetkids.com
© Lonely Planet 2021

Printed in Singapore
10 9 8 7 6 5 4 3 2 1

STAY IN TOUCH
lonelyplanet.com/contact

Lonely Planet Office:
IRELAND
Digital Depot, Roe Lane (off Thomas St), Digital Hub, Dublin 8, D08 TCV4

World Tour

Contents

World Tour

Let's travel around the world to discover some of the most amazing places on Earth. There are seven continents to explore, each home to a wide range of landscapes, wildlife, and fascinating cultures. Get ready for bustling cities, mighty mountains, sweeping grasslands, and hostile deserts as we embark on an epic world tour.

North America

Let's begin in North America, Earth's third-largest continent, containing the United States of America, Canada, and Mexico, as well as the countries of Central America and the Caribbean. Mexico City is the largest city in North America and Denali, in Alaska, is its highest mountain.

Equator An imaginary line around Earth's middle that separates the planet into northern and southern hemispheres

South America

Next stop is South America, the fourth-largest continent, stretching from just above the Equator right down almost to the Antarctic. There are 12 countries here, the biggest of which is Brazil. The Amazon, the world's largest river by volume, flows here, surrounded by the world's largest rain forest.

Europe

Europe may be the second-smallest continent but around one quarter of the world's people live here. Its land stretches from Scandinavia in the north to warmer Mediterranean countries farther south. Moscow, in Russia, is the continent's largest city and the Vatican City, in Italy, is its smallest country.

Asia

Asia is the world's largest continent, and is home to more people than all the others. Its largest city, Tokyo, in Japan, has more people than the whole of Canada! The Himalayas, the world's highest mountain range, spreads across the middle of the continent.

Australasia

This is the smallest continental region in the world. Its islands, including Australia and New Zealand, have been cut off from other continents for so long that there are animals living here, like red kangaroos, that are found nowhere else on Earth.

Africa

Africa is the second-largest continent and has 54 countries, which is more than any other. The River Nile, the world's longest river, runs through east Africa, heading north toward the Mediterranean Sea in Egypt. Africa is also home to the largest hot desert on Earth—the Sahara.

Antarctica

Surrounded by the Southern Ocean, Antarctica is nearly double the size of Australia. The land is covered by a thick layer of ice, and less rain falls here than in any other continent. It is the only continent on Earth where people have never permanently lived.

North America

There's so much to explore in North America, from the world's largest freshwater lake, Lake Superior, to the world's largest island, Greenland, and the world's hottest place, Death Valley. The continent's biggest country, Canada, covers much of the frozen north. To the south, tropical forests stretch across the countries of Central America and the islands of the Caribbean.

Get ready to spot grizzly bears in the Alaskan wilderness, glimpse movie stars in Hollywood, and dive with sea otters in the Californian kelp forests. Arrive in Mexico City just in time to celebrate the Day of the Dead. Then, at the southernmost tip of the continent, look out for toucans and monkeys in the tropical rain forests of Costa Rica.

Denali National Park
Alaska, USA

Montréal
Québec, Canada

Banff National Park
Alberta, Canada

Mojave Desert
Nevada, USA

Rocky Mountains
Montana, USA

Hollywood
California, USA

New York City
New York, USA

Kelp Forests
California, USA

Havana
Cuba

Mexico City
Mexico

Corcovado Rain Forest
Costa Rica

DENALI NATIONAL PARK

First stop is Alaska, the USA's most northerly and coldest state. It's also its largest—bigger than the next three largest states combined. At its center is Denali National Park, a vast wilderness of mountains, rivers, and glaciers, packed with wildlife.

Moose

One—The number of roads in the national park, the Denali Park Road, which winds for 82 miles (148 km).

Brown Bear: There are around 300–350 wild brown bears, or grizzlies, living in the national park.

Golden eagle

20,310 ft (6,190 m)—the height of the tallest peak in the USA, Denali, which gives the park its name.

The name "Denali" means "The High One" in the local Native American language.

100,000—the number of icy glaciers flowing (slowly!) through Alaska.

Mammals: Nearly 40 different species of mammals roam the park, including moose, Dall sheep, and grizzly bears.

Walk on the Wild Side: Denali National Park covers a huge area, larger than the US state of New Hampshire. This vast wilderness offers a wide range of outdoor activities, including hiking, climbing, cross-country skiing, dog-sledding, and riding in snowmobiles.

Ocean Giants: Try your luck whale watching off the coast of Alaska. Humpback whales, black-and-white orcas, and smaller minke whales can be spotted here.

Mountaineers: Dall sheep are nimble climbers. They live on steep slopes and mountainous ridges near rugged terrain.

NEW YORK CITY

Filled with people, traffic, and towering skyscrapers, New York is the USA's biggest city. People can get away from the noise and bustle in Central Park, which has miles of cycling tracks, open spaces, ponds, and trees. Central Park is the most visited park in the USA.

Vintage Carousel: This popular tourist attraction was first built in 1871. The original carousel was powered by a real horse!

38 million—the number of visitors to Central Park in a year, making it the most visited park in the USA.

26—the number of baseball fields in Central Park.

Times Square: Just south of the park, Times Square is one of the world's most famous city squares. Lined with shops, attractions, and dazzling neon signs, it draws around 50 million visitors a year. The lights here are so bright, they can even be seen from space!

Piercing the Clouds: Hundreds of tall, narrow skyscrapers make up the skyline around Central Park.

Statue of Liberty: This 305-ft- (93-m-) tall statue stands on an island in New York Harbor. A gift to the USA from France, it was assembled in 1886 from 350 separate pieces.

HOTDOGS

1,000—the number of hot dogs eaten in New York City every minute.

Tuck In: Food carts scattered throughout the park sell hot dogs, pretzels, cookies, and sodas—yum!

CASTLE ZOO

AMUSEMENT PARK PLAYGROUND

Central Park is a popular place for cycling, jogging, and playing sports. There are 12 tennis courts, four basketball courts, and six football pitches.

Central Park Zoo: At the park's zoo, you can see snow leopards, puffins, penguins, sea lions, and many other animals.

BANFF NATIONAL PARK

Banff National Park is the oldest national park in Canada, set within North America's Rocky Mountains. The park is known for its scenic roads and breathtaking rail routes. Among turquoise lakes, dense forests, and snowy peaks, there is an abundance of wildlife to spot.

Over three million people visit the national park every year to enjoy hiking, climbing, skiing, and camping.

.... Puma

Flying Squirrel: These furry rodents can be spotted soaring through Banff's trees by moonlight. They have huge eyes to help them see in the dark and can glide over 300 ft (90 m).

1,000 miles (1,600 km)— the total length of hiking trails.

Wolf .....

Roaming Wildlife: Big-horn sheep, deer, bears, wild cats, and birds of prey are all found living in the national park.

: Brown bear

Alberta, Canada

Kestrel .....

Birdwatching: There are over 260 species of birds living around the national park, from small song birds to giant birds of prey.

Chugging Along: The Rocky Mountaineer train travels between Vancouver and Banff, giving passengers spectacular mountain views.

Yellow ..... **warbler**

365 mi (587 km)— the length of the Bow River which runs through Banff.

Icefields Parkway: Known as one of the most scenic drives in the world, this winding road stretches 140 miles (230 km).

Bighorn sheep

White-tailed deer

Lynx

Bald Eagle: With a 7-ft (2-m) wingspan, the bald eagle is one of the largest birds of prey in the world. Banff is one of the best places to spot bald eagles, which nest near rivers and lakes in the national park.

MONTRÉAL

Montréal is the largest city in Québec and the second-largest city in Canada. It is known for its vast parks and ice-cold winters. During the coldest months, the city becomes a winter wonderland and a popular base for people to take part in a range of exciting winter sports.

Parlez-Vous Français?:
Most people living in Montréal speak French as their first or second language.

The city of Montréal is situated on a huge island. Its name, "Mont Real" means "Royal Mountain" in French.

Ski Snack:
A popular food in Montréal is "poutine," which is cheesy French fries topped with gravy.

Eager Beaver: The beaver is the national animal of Canada and the largest rodent in the country, measuring 4 ft (1.3 m) from snout to tail. Beavers have thick fur, webbed feet, and a flattened paddle-like tail.

Deep Freeze: Montréal gets very cold in winter. In 1957, the temperature plummeted to a record low of -37.8 °C (-36 °F), and the added wind chill can make it feel even colder!

60 days—the average number of days that it snows in Montréal each year.

Summer Scorcher: It's not always cold here. During the summer, Montréal gets hot and humid, with temperatures reaching a sticky 86 °F (30 °C).

Snow Sports: As well as skiing, there's ice skating, tubing, fat tire biking, snowshoeing, hockey, and dog sledding to enjoy. The world's first indoor ice hockey game was held in Montréal in 1875.

275—the number of ice skating rinks there are in Montréal.

17

ROCKY MOUNTAINS

The great range known as the Rocky Mountains stretches from Western Canada down into the USA. On the border between the two countries lies Glacier National Park. Here, you'll find the beautiful Swiftcurrent Lake, where visitors can go hiking and take scenic boat rides.

Over three million people visit Glacier National Park every year to go camping, cycling, fishing, and canoeing, and to explore hundreds of miles of hiking trails.

5,000—the approximate number of moose living in Montana.

Cattle Ranching: Ranches in Montana farm animals, like cows and sheep, for food. They are herded by cowgirls or cowboys on horseback and rounded up with a loop of rope called a lasso.

Grinnell Point is a pyramid-shaped mountain that rises sharply above Swiftcurrent Lake.

Patterned Ducks: Harlequin ducks like choppy water and live near fast-moving mountain streams.

76 million years ago— when the Rocky Mountains were formed.

3,000 miles (4,800 km)— the distance that the Rocky Mountains stretch.

0.7 sq miles (1.8 sq km)— the size of Blackfoot Glacier, which is the biggest of the 26 glaciers left in Glacier National Park.

A yellow wildflower called a glacier lily grows on mountain slopes and in the park's green meadows.

Shaggy Mountain Goat: Found on the Rocky Mountains' slopes, these agile creatures are expert climbers. They can tackle steep slopes and leap as far as 12 feet (4 m).

HOLLYWOOD

Los Angeles is the second-largest city in the USA, situated on the West Coast of America. Hollywood is a famous area of the city where America's film industry has been based since the days of silent movies. Here, people love to visit the Hollywood Walk of Fame where the biggest stars of the movie world are celebrated.

Award-winning: The first Oscars ceremony was staged in Hollywood in 1929.

On the Bright Side: Los Angeles sees around 292 days of sunshine every year.

The Chinese Theatre on the Hollywood Walk of Fame is one of the most sought-after venues for glittering movie premieres.

Starstruck: The Walk of Fame on Hollywood Boulevard features over 2,600 shiny star-shaped plaques celebrating famous actors, directors, producers, and musicians.

1912—the year that Paramount Pictures opened, making it the longest operating film studio in Hollywood.

The iconic Hollywood sign on Hollywood Hills was originally built in 1923 to advertise land for sale. Today, visitors can hike, horse-ride, or take a helicopter ride over the hillside.

Glitzy : Hollywood has earned the showy nickname "Tinseltown."

Lights, Camera, Action!: Universal Studios is a theme park in Los Angeles that is also a working movie studio. Here, visitors can glimpse behind the scenes of big blockbuster films and take photos on famous film sets.

KELP FORESTS

Giant kelp is a seaweed that grows in dense forests that stretch for hundreds of miles along the West Coast of America. This mega seaweed can grow to 100 ft (30 m) tall, forming vast undersea jungles that provide homes for sea otters, gray whales, and many species of fish.

Giant kelp can grow around 10 in (30 cm) per day and live up to seven years. It grows best in cool, clear, nutrient-rich water.

..... Harbor seal

Fluffy Coats:
Sea otters have the thickest fur of any animal, which keeps them warm in the cold ocean water.

A host of creatures, including fish, snails, sea stars, seals, and sharks, rely on kelp forests for food and shelter.

...... Sea urchin

Hold Tight: Kelp doesn't have roots, instead it has a root-like "holdfast" that anchors it to the seabed.

Small to Big: A large area of kelp is called a kelp forest, while a smaller area is called a kelp bed.

Fishing for Food: Diving birds, like cormorants and terns, plunge down into the water from above to spear fish with their sharp beaks.

Sun-seekers: Kelp has bubble-like "gas bladders," that keep it afloat as it grows up toward the sun.

Not Just a Furry Face: Sea otters shelter within the giant kelp and help to keep the forests healthy. The otters eat crabs, sea urchins, and other invertebrates using rocks to crack open their shells.

Octopus

Natural Balance: Sea urchins chomp through kelp at a rapid rate, and sea otters feast on the urchins in turn.

Sea star

THE MOJAVE DESERT

The Mojave Desert is the smallest and driest of four deserts in the USA. Stretching across southern Nevada and southeastern California, the desert is known for its sparse vegetation, rugged peaks, and arid valleys. Here, lizards and squirrels scurry across the sand, spiders and scorpions stalk their prey, and coyotes and rabbits hide in underground burrows.

Prickly cacti survive the harsh, dry conditions by storing water inside them for long periods of time. Many types of cacti have large, colorful flowers that burst into bloom in spring.

129 °F (54 °C)—the hottest temperature ever recorded on Earth, in the Mojave Desert's Death Valley.

Gambel's quail

Mule deer

Ground squirrel

Lizard

Scorpion ......

Red-knee tarantula

Many desert animals escape the fierce daytime heat by hiding below ground.

Sleep Tight: Some animals hibernate to avoid extreme heat and drought, waking up to drink when it rains.

Coyote

Rattlesnake....

Desert Scavengers: The turkey vulture is one of the largest birds in North America. It has a massive wingspan of 6 ft (1.8 m) and a red, featherless head.

Costa's Hummingbird: This tiny, energetic bird is less than 3.5 in (9 cm) in length. It feeds on the nectar produced by flowering cacti plants.

Monarch Butterfly: During their seasonal migration from the USA to Mexico, monarch butterflies travel roughly 3,000 miles (4,800 km). They stop at the Mojave Desert to eat the milkweed plants, their favorite food, that grow here.

⋯⋯ Costa's Hummingbird

⋯⋯ Desert tortoise

⋯⋯ Black-tailed jackrabbit

6 in (15 cm)—the amount of rain that the Mojave Desert receives in a year.

Coyotes: Quick on their feet, coyotes hunt for desert rabbits, birds, and snakes, but they also eat cacti fruit. Coyotes live in underground dens and "sing" to communicate with each other.

MEXICO CITY

Mexico City is built on the ruins of the former capital of the Aztec Empire and is one of the oldest and largest cities in the Americas. Mexico is known for its ancient civilizations, including the Olmecs, the Maya, and the city of Teotihuacan. In early November, Mexico City celebrates the Day of the Dead, where people dress up and take part in colorful parades.

Day of the Dead: On November 1 and 2, the people of Mexico hold a celebration to pay respect to their ancestors.

Deadly Dress-up: Thousands of people wear costumes, gather for music and dancing, and take part in street parades.

Waking the Dead: People wear shells and other noisy objects that clatter while they dance.

Spooky Sweets: On the Day of the Dead, sugar skulls called *calaveras* are decorated and used as offerings to the dead.

20 million—the number of visitors per year to Our Lady of Guadalupe, a church and shrine in Mexico City.

Mexican Feast: Chocolate, pumpkins, and avocados all originated in Mexico.

Pyramids of Teotihuacan: The city of Teotihuacan was built over 2,000 years ago just north of Mexico City, but was abandoned in around 500 CE. Some of its buildings remain standing, including two giant pyramids dedicated to the Moon (left) and the Sun (right).

During the Day of the Dead, dressing up is all part of the fun. Some people wear skeleton costumes and paint skulls on their faces. Others wear long, flowing dresses made of colorful lace.

CORCOVADO RAIN FOREST

In Central America, Costa Rica is sandwiched between the Caribbean Sea and the Pacific Ocean. With sandy beaches, chattering jungles, and mighty volcanoes, there is plenty to explore. Around 20 percent of the country is covered by forests—including the dense Corcovado Rain Forest in the southwest—and there are 30 protected national parks and reserves full of incredible wildlife.

200 in (500 cm)— the amount of rain that the rain forests receive in a year.

Keel-billed toucan ....

250—the number of species of mammal living here, from wild cats to white-faced capuchin monkeys.

Squirrel monkey

Costa Rica is one of the most biodiverse places in the world with around 500,000 species, including six types of toucan and 10 percent of the world's butterflies.

Scarlet macaw

Red-eyed tree frog

Flora and Fauna: The forest contains 200 species of trees, 9,000 kinds of flowering plants, and 1,400 species of just one flower—the orchid.

Squirrel Monkeys: These small monkeys are social animals that live in groups, called troops, and can be very noisy. Up to 100 squirrel monkeys live in a troop.

Heavy rains encourage ferns, fungi, and vines to grow, carpeting the canopy.

White-faced capuchin

200—the number of reptile species living in the jungle, most of which are snakes, alongside around 150 species of frogs and toads.

Turtles: Four species of turtle nest on Costa Rica's beaches, including huge green sea turtles, which can lay up to 700 eggs in one season. Once hatched, the baby turtles rush as fast as they can down to the sea.

Look Up: Numerous animals, including squirrel monkeys and scarlet macaws, make their homes in the canopy.

HAVANA

Dating back to the 16th century, Havana is the capital and largest city of Cuba, which is the largest country in the Caribbean by both area and population. The city is best known for its tropical climate, historic monuments, lively culture, and classic cars.

Many of the city's oldest buildings date back to the 16th century, when the Spanish founded Old Havana. Buildings are decorated with bright, pastel colors and eye-catching designs.

60,000—the number of vintage American cars in Cuba, some of which are battered, while others are beautifully restored.

Plaza de Armas: Lined with royal palm trees, elegant buildings and a fortress that was built hundreds of years ago, Plaza de Armas is the oldest and busiest square in Havana.

Cuba

Fun and Games: Baseball is the most popular sport in Cuba. Dominoes is also a favorite pastime.

Swinging Sounds: "Son" is a traditional genre of music that originated in Cuba. This joyous style mixes lively rhythms with classical guitar and is played by live bands all over Havana.

1577—the year that Havana's fortress was built above the harbor to protect the city from invading pirates (a common problem back then!).

Classic Cuba: Vintage cars in all shades of the rainbow line the streets of Havana. Most of these are American imports that date back to the 1950s or earlier. There are no new American cars because the USA banned exports of its cars (and lots of other things) when Cuba became a communist country in 1959. Classic cars are popular with tourists looking for a traditional ride.

South America

From the tropical north to its windswept southern tip, South America features many extraordinary habitats. In the north of the continent, the Amazon Rain Forest teems with life. Farther south, the forest gives way to open grasslands. Between the Pacific Ocean and the Andes Mountains is the Atacama Desert, the driest hot desert in the world.

Spot rare pink river dolphins along the Amazon River, surrounded by lush tropical rain forest; soak up the sun on the beaches of Rio de Janeiro, or dance the samba in the world's largest carnival. In Peru, explore the ancient hillside ruins of Machu Picchu, then, watch distant planets and stars in the clear-skied Atacama Desert.

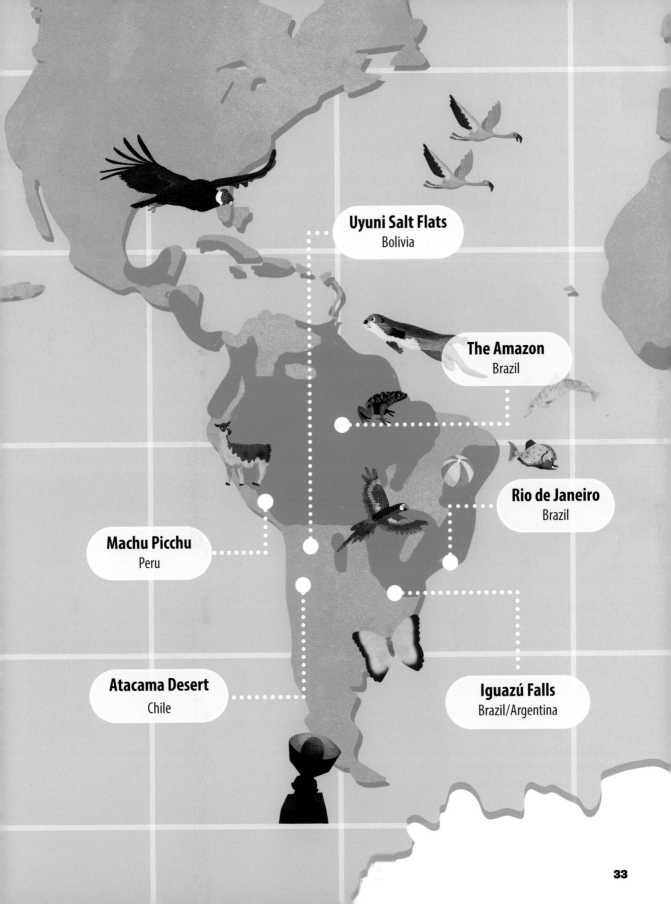

Uyuni Salt Flats
Bolivia

The Amazon
Brazil

Rio de Janeiro
Brazil

Machu Picchu
Peru

Atacama Desert
Chile

Iguazú Falls
Brazil/Argentina

RIO DE JANEIRO

Known as "Rio" for short, Rio de Janeiro is a seaside city in southeast Brazil that overlooks a large, scenic bay. The city draws millions of visitors to its huge sandy beaches, nearby islands, and lively annual carnival, which is the biggest in the world.

During the five-day carnival, locals celebrate with street parties, costumes, and elaborate parades.

5 million—the number of local people that gather in the streets to celebrate the carnival.

World Cup Winners: Brazil has won the men's soccer World Cup five times—that's more than any other nation.

Carnival King: At each carnival, someone is crowned "King Momo," the mystical jester who is supposed to lead the festivities.

173,850—the number of spectators at a World Cup game in Rio in 1950, which is a world record.

Carnival Countdown:
There are 70 Samba clubs in Rio where people get together to make festive floats and costumes, and practice dance routines, in preparation for the annual carnival events.

Playing Ball:
Rio's sandy beaches are a hive of activity with groups of people playing volleyball, soccer, and frescobol in the sun.

Christ the Redeemer Statue:
You can't miss this 98-ft- (30-m-) tall statue of Jesus Christ that sits atop Corcovado Mountain, dominating the city skyline. It gets struck by lightning several times a year!

2.5 miles (4 km)—the length of Rio's world-famous Copacabana Beach.

Portuguese explorers named Rio de Janeiro in 1502. The name means "River of January"—it is thought that the explorers mistook the bay for a river.

THE AMAZON

The Amazon is the largest intact rain forest in the world. It extends across nine South American countries and covers around two-thirds of Brazil. The immense Amazon River flows through the rain forest, providing habitats for a whole host of creatures. Countless amazing creatures, including tapirs, poison-dart frogs, and piranhas, make their homes here.

10 percent— the proportion of all known plant and animal species that live in the Amazon.

Anaconda Snake: There are more than 370 types of reptile in the Amazon, including the anaconda, which grows up to 30 ft (9 m) long and is one of the largest snakes in the world.

40,000—the number of different plant species in the Amazon, while the number of insect species is in the millions!

Giant Otter: These sociable animals like to stick together, living in groups of up to 20 animals. They live in rivers across the Amazon and mainly eat fish, but they have been known to attack larger prey, even anacondas! Giant otters are the largest otters in the world.

Rare Wildlife: The Amazon is one of Earth's few remaining habitats for the pink river dolphin, also known as a "boto."

Sloths: These slow and steady creatures spend most of their time in the trees. They have very poor eyesight, which may be why they move so slowly, but a powerful sense of smell. Sloths can swim three times faster than they move on land.

Toco toucan

Macaw Parrots: There are 17 species of macaw in the Amazon Rain Forest. Macaws have vibrant feathers, long, elegant tails, and strong beaks that they use to crack nuts and eat salty clay from the riverbank. These birds can live to be 60 years old.

Tapir

Poison-dart frog

Fierce Hunters: Jaguars are the largest cats in South America and incredibly strong for their size. They hunt in the day and night, and can take down huge creatures like caimans with one powerful bite.

In the last 40 years, the Brazilian Amazon has lost over 18 percent of its rain forest to illegal logging and agriculture. That's about the size of California.

4,000 miles (6,400 km)— the length of the winding Amazon River.

Electric Eels: Despite the name, electric eels are more closely related to carp and catfish than eels. They can deliver a powerful electric shock, which is used to stun their prey.

Red-bellied piranha

IGUAZÚ FALLS

Stretching for 1.7 miles (2.7 km) along the border between Argentina and Brazil, the tumbling cascades of Iguazú Falls are one of South America's most awe-inspiring natural wonders. Surrounded by lush rain forest and protected by two national parks, the falls are home to incredible plants and wildlife.

269 ft (82 m)—the height of the tallest waterfall, known as the Devil's Throat.

Big Butterflies: The blue morpho butterfly is one of 635 species of butterfly that live here. With a wingspan of up to 8 in (20 cm), the blue morpho is one of the biggest butterflies in the world.

Enough water to fill five Olympic swimming pools can tumble over the falls every second!

Caiman

1.5 million—the number of visitors to Iguazú Falls each year.

Golden parakeet

275—the number of individual waterfalls that make up the falls, together creating one of the largest waterfalls in the world.

Hyacinth macaw

Toothless Giants: With their long, sticky tongues, giant anteaters swallow around 35,000 ants and termites every day! Anteaters have a sense of smell that is 40 times stronger than that of a human.

Floating Down the River: Visitors can take a boat trip or go white-water rafting near the falls. Surrounded by the roar of the waterfall, and with macaws and toucans flying overhead, it's sure to be a memorable trip.

Nature Spotting: There are many animals to look out for near Iguazú Falls, from tapirs and giant anteaters that root around at ground level, to climbing squirrel monkeys and sharp-toothed caimans.

Squirrel monkey

Tapir

Giant anteater

MACHU PICCHU

High up in the Andes Mountains of Peru is the ancient stone city of Machu Picchu. Situated on a narrow ridge 7,972 ft (2,430 m) above sea level, Machu Picchu overlooks the Urubamba River and is surrounded by the steep mountain slopes. This fascinating ruin is one of the best-preserved cities of the ancient Inca Empire.

Incan Fortress: Machu Picchu was built in 1450 CE by the Inca civilization. Many of the ancient city's dry-stone walls and buildings still stand today.

7,972 ft (2,430 m)—the height above sea level of La Ciudadela (the Citadel) at the heart of the city.

32,592 hectares—the size of the ancient city, taking in rugged mountain slopes and green valleys.

Llamas: Woolly llamas are native to South America and have been kept for food, and to carry heavy loads, for centuries in the Andes. Llamas are related to camels, but without humps, and can grow to 6 ft (1.8 m) tall.

Lost and Found: Machu Picchu was abandoned in the 16th century after the Spanish invasion and wasn't discovered again by the outside world until 1911. The site became a protected UNESCO World Heritage site in 1983.

Giant Gliders: The Andean Condor lives in the Andes Mountains and can be seen soaring above Machu Picchu. With a wingspan of 10 ft (3 m), it is one of the world's largest birds.

"Machu Picchu" means "Old Mountain" in the indigenous Quechua Indian language.

The structures were built using a technique called *ashlar*, where stones are cut to size and placed without mortar. The Inca people were masters at this technique—even a knife blade couldn't fit between two stones.

THE ATACAMA DESERT

The Atacama Desert is the world's oldest desert and one of the driest places on Earth. It stretches around 600 miles (1,000 km) across Chile, between the Pacific coast and the Andes Mountains. The desert is full of unusual rock formations and, unlike many deserts, temperatures in the Atacama stay relatively mild throughout the year.

330—the number of cloud-free nights that the Atacama Desert sees each year.

0.04-0.12 in (1-3 mm)—the amount of rain that the driest part of the desert receives in a year.

Super Dry: There are parts of the Atacama Desert where no rain has been recorded for hundreds of years!

With some parts over 16,400 ft (5,000 m) high, the Atacama Desert plateau is one of the best places in the world to watch the night skies. It is from here that the Atacama Large Millimeter Array (ALMA)—the world's most powerful observatory of its kind—has been positioned to study the Universe.

The dry air, cloudless skies, high altitude, and lack of light pollution make the Atacama Desert an unbeatable place to stargaze.

Prickly Plants: Cacti have adapted to survive the harsh climate by storing water for long periods of time, but few other plants survive here.

Atacama Large Millimeter Array: This giant observatory is made up of a group of 66 powerful radio antennae ("array" means "group"), each around 40 ft (12 m) wide. The array is used to spot faraway galaxies and look for new planets. ALMA is so accurate, it could spot a golf ball 9 miles (15 km) away!

UYUNI SALT FLATS

In southwest Bolivia, near the high peaks of the Andes Mountains, is a vast, salt-crusted expanse called the Uyuni Salt Flats. This magical landscape was created thousands of years ago, when prehistoric lakes dried up, leaving the largest area of salt flats in the world.

10 billion tons—the estimated amount of salt contained in the salt flats.

4,000 sq miles (10,500 sq km)—the size of the salt flats, making them the largest in the world.

During the rainy season, between December and April, a thin layer of water collects on the salt, transforming the landscape into the world's largest natural mirror.

The endless white plains and flat horizon provide strange and funny photo opportunities. Visitors can take double photos of themselves on the super-reflective surface when the salt is wet.

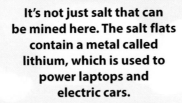

It's not just salt that can be mined here. The salt flats contain a metal called lithium, which is used to power laptops and electric cars.

15 percent—the amount of the world's lithium reserves thought to be stored beneath the salt crust.

33 ft (10 m)—the depth of the salt at its deepest.

All to Themselves: The conditions are so harsh that very few animals can live on the salt flats. But no fewer than three different species of flamingo thrive here.

Flamingos: Within the salt flats is a deep red lake called Laguna Colorado where huge flocks of flamingos come to feed on plankton. Both the lake and the flamingos get their color from the red-colored algae in the water.

Europe

Europe shares the same landmass as Asia, stretching from the cold Arctic north to the warm Mediterranean Sea in the south. There are over 40 countries in Europe and most of them have a mild, temperate climate with warm summers and cool winters.

Take a tour of London's most famous attractions on board an iconic red bus, or watch the world go by from an elegant Parisian café. Strap into skis and race down the slopes of the Swiss Alps, or travel south to dive with dolphins in the warm waters of the Algarve. On Europe's eastern edge, go ice-skating in Moscow's grand Red Square or visit the city's ancient fortress, the Kremlin.

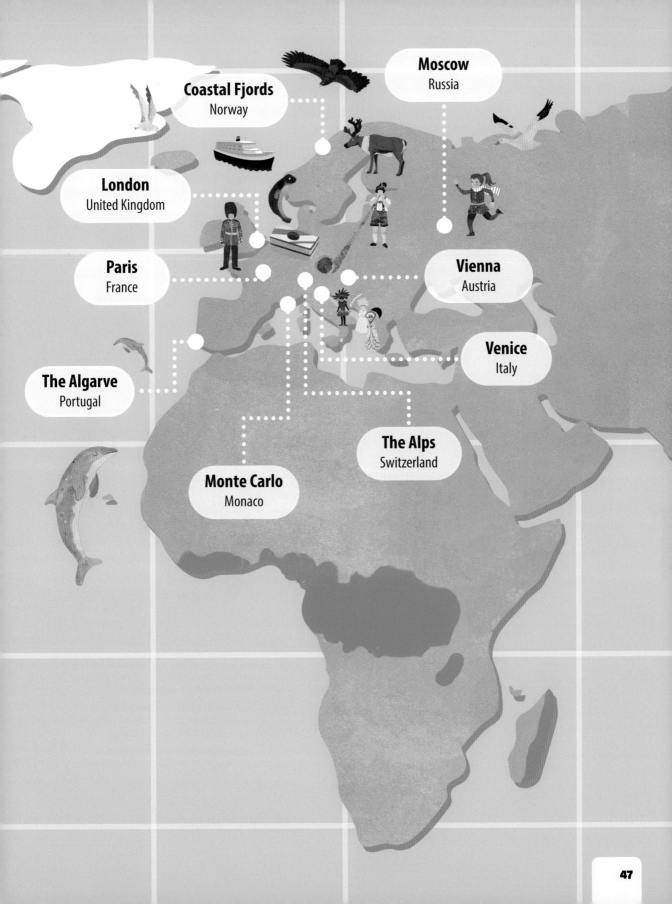

Coastal Fjords
Norway

Moscow
Russia

London
United Kingdom

Paris
France

Vienna
Austria

Venice
Italy

The Algarve
Portugal

The Alps
Switzerland

Monte Carlo
Monaco

COASTAL FJORDS

Norway is a Scandinavian country in northern Europe, bordered by the North Atlantic Ocean. Visitors come from far and wide to see Norway's majestic fjords, where deep channels of blue seawater cut into the rugged landscape. This striking scenery was formed by giant glaciers during Earth's ice ages, millions of years ago.

Porpoises: Seen in shallow fjords, harbor porpoises are the smallest members of the whale family. They can dive up to 660 ft (200 m) deep, and come up for air every 25 seconds.

Creatures of the North: Reindeer, seals, and soaring birds of prey make their homes here in the cool northern climate.

Reindeer

127 miles (205 km)— the length of the longest fjord, which is also the deepest, descending down to 4,291 ft (1,308 m) deep.

Saltwater Channels: A fjord is a deep, narrow extension of the sea that cuts into the land. Steep rocky banks line the water's edge.

Harbor seal ················

Golden eagle ....

300—the number of Norwegian mountains that are taller than 6,600 ft (2,000 m), some of which are so steep that no one has ever tried to climb them!

Sami Reindeer Herders: The Sami people are indigenous to northern Norway and have lived here, and in Sweden, Finland, and Russia, for thousands of years. They are nomadic people who often migrate with large herds of reindeer. Reindeer are essential to the Sami way of life, providing food, clothing, and tools.

White-tailed Eagles: With a wingspan of 9 ft (2.7 m), white-tailed eagles are among the largest birds in the world. They can be seen gliding above the water and swooping down to pluck out fish.

1,000—the number of fjords along the coastline of Norway.

On the Water: One of the best ways to explore the fjords is by boat. Visitors can travel on all kinds of watercrafts, from little motorboats that venture through narrow waterways, to large cruise ships that explore the coastline.

LONDON

At the bustling heart of London, the UK's biggest city, is Buckingham Palace—home to the British Royal family. The palace is surrounded by parkland and looks out onto The Mall, a historic road that runs between the palace and Trafalgar Square. During the summer, visitors can get a glimpse of the palace's lavish rooms on special tours.

1 million—the number of people that gathered in The Mall outside Buckingham Palace to watch the Golden Jubilee in 2002, which celebrated the Queen's 50th anniversary on the throne.

The Tower of London: This historic fortress has been used as a palace and a prison by past kings and queens. The Crown Jewels are kept here under armed guard, including the Imperial State Crown which contains 2,868 diamonds!

300—the number of languages spoken in London, the highest number of any city in the world!

United Kingdom

Fit for a Queen: Buckingham Palace has been the official London home for the British royal family since 1837 when Britain's longest-reigning monarch, Queen Victoria, moved in.

775—the number of rooms inside Buckingham Palace, including 52 royal and guest bedrooms and 78 bathrooms.

London Bus: London's iconic buses have been painted red since 1907. Today there are around 9,000 buses calling at 19,000 bus stops.

Changing the Guard: This daily ceremony sees the handover between guards and lasts 45 minutes.

Party Time: Every year, 8,000 people are invited to the Queen's Summer Garden Party. Thankfully she's got the space to fit them all in. The party takes place in the palace garden, the largest private garden in London.

PARIS

Paris is the capital city of France in Western Europe. The city is famous for its beautiful architecture, fascinating museums and galleries, and fashionable shops. Parisians are known for their love of coffee and fine food, so there are plenty of lively cafés and restaurants across the city to choose from.

Around 10 billion baguettes are eaten in France every year! Patisseries (French bakeries) are popular across Paris, selling baguettes, croissants, and elegant cakes.

6,000—the number of streets in Paris, with some only a few feet long!

10 million—the number of visitors to The Louvre in a year, making it the most visited museum in the world.

100 years—the amount of time that it took to build Paris' famous Notre Dame Cathedral.

The Tour de France: Every year, the world's most famous cycling event takes place in France, involving cyclists from many different countries. It takes 23 days to complete, making The Tour de France one of the most challenging cycling races in the world. The race ends in Paris on a famous street called the Champs-Élysées.

Symbol of the City: Built in 1889, the Eiffel Tower is 1,063 ft (324 m) tall and has 1,700 steps, which are climbed by millions of visitors each year.

20 years— the amount of time that the Eiffel Tower was supposed to stand—that was over 130 years ago!

BOULANGERIE

METROPOLI

Café Culture: The tradition of gathering in cafés goes back hundreds of years, when the artists and writers of Paris would meet to share their work and ideas. The city's cafés remain popular places to sit and watch the world go by to this day.

53

THE ALPS

Situated in the center of Europe, Switzerland is one of the most mountainous countries in the world. With ice-blue lakes sat between snow-capped mountains, Switzerland is a popular place for outdoor activities like hiking, climbing, and cycling. When winter arrives, visitors travel from around the world to ski and snowboard at famous resorts in the Swiss Alps.

60 percent—the amount of Switzerland that is covered by mountains.

Famous Foods: As one of the first countries to produce milk chocolate, Switzerland is now famous for making some of the most delicious chocolate in the world.

The Alphorn: Blowing into this giant wooden instrument makes a deep, round sound that was historically used to call cows at milking time. The alphorn is now played as part of traditional Swiss folk music.

Ski Season: One of the world's best places for skiing is at Zermatt in the Swiss Alps. The resort has the highest ski runs in Europe at 12,500 ft (3,800 m). From here, you can ski downhill for an exhilarating 13 miles (21 km) on one of the world's longest ski runs.

Breaking Records: The Charles Kuonen Suspension Bridge is the world's longest pedestrian suspension bridge. It stretches nearly 1,600 ft (500 m) and provides views of the Matterhorn and surrounding mountains.

Mountain Giant: The Matterhorn is one of the tallest mountains in Switzerland. It has a jagged pyramid-shaped peak that is 14,692 ft (4,478 m) high.

Mountain Call: Yodelling was invented by shepherds as a way to communicate with each other across the mountains. This song-like call now forms an important part of Swiss folk music.

Peak in the Meadow: The name "Matterhorn" means "Peak in the Meadow" as the mountain rises sharply above its surrounding grassy slopes.

On Top of the World: At 11,332 ft (3,454 m) above sea level, the Jungfraujoch in the Swiss Alps is the highest railway station in Europe. Stopping here, travelers are greeted by snow underfoot, mountains all around, and views over a nearby glacier.

MONTE CARLO

Situated on the sunny southeast coast of France, Monaco is a tiny country known for its lavish parties, designer shops, and wealthy residents. Monte Carlo is the central region of Monaco that stretches along the seafront, facing the Mediterranean Sea. This is where famous events like the Monaco Yacht Show and the Monaco Grand Prix take place every year, drawing thousands of spectators.

2.4 miles (3.83 km)—the length of Monaco's Mediterranean coastline, with the whole country roughly the same size as Central Park in New York.

LES VOITURES

Racing Cars: First hosted in 1929, the Monaco Formula 1 Grand Prix is one of the most famous racing events in the world. The circuit is difficult and often dangerous, made up of tight corners and narrow roads.

Super-sized: The Monaco Yacht Show is the biggest superyacht event in Europe. Huge, lavish yachts arrive from around the world, some of which are over 300 ft (100 m) long.

78—the number of laps drivers must complete in the Grand Prix for a total distance of 162 miles (260 km).

The legendary casino at Monte Carlo is an ornate building covered in statues, where people come to spend lots of money on gambling.

Flash the Cash: Monte Carlo's opulent shopping center is packed with designer and luxury stores catering to the rich and famous.

Underwater World: At Monaco's famous Oceanographic Museum, visitors can marvel at 6,000 species of sea creature and explore vast ocean-related displays. The historic building sits on a sheer cliff overlooking the Mediterranean Sea.

12,000— the number of millionaires who live in Monaco, which is nearly a third of the country's population!

VIENNA

Vienna is the capital and largest city in Austria, a landlocked country in central Europe. It is known for its historic old town, impressive museums, and busy music scene. Famous concert venues, such as the Vienna State Opera House, stage spectacular (and sometimes unusual) performances all year round.

Vienna's Vegetable Orchestra plays concerts around the world using a range of fresh vegetables as instruments. The audience are then offered vegetable soup at the end of the show.

Unfamiliar Sounds: Carrots, leeks and pumpkins make good instruments!

Playing to the Crowds: The Vienna State Opera House can seat over 1,700 people in its grand auditorium. More than 60 different opera and ballet performances play here each year.

Giant Ferris Wheel: Vienna's famous Ferris wheel has been standing for over 100 years. It is 213 ft (65 m) tall, giving passengers a bird's-eye view of the city and the Danube River flowing below. Individual cabins can be booked for special occasions with an incredible view!

Music and Dancing: Hundreds of magnificent balls are held in Vienna every year.

Step in Time: The Viennese Waltz is a traditional style of ballroom dancing where couples move in time with the music.

Music in the Garden: Each year, around 100,000 people watch the Summer Night Concert, where some of the best musicians in Austria perform in a beautiful outdoor setting.

VENICE

Built in a lagoon containing around 120 small islands, Venice is known as "The Floating City." Here, networks of canals act as roads and people use boats to get around. The biggest canal is the Grand Canal, which runs through the heart of the city. In February, the city erupts into celebration during the famous Venice Carnival.

The Grand Canal: Venice's busiest waterway snakes through the city. It is lined with grand palaces that are hundreds of years old.

Gondolas: These traditional flat-bottomed boats have been used to ferry people along Venice's canals since the 16th century. There are around 400 still operating today.

Party Time: Since 1162 the Venice Carnival has brought the city to life with loud and colorful celebrations. People dress up in extravagant costumes and wear traditional Venetian masks.

The Rialto Bridge was the first bridge to be built over the Grand Canal, and still the most famous. The bridge has been standing for over 500 years.

0.04-0.08 in (1-2 mm)— the amount that Venice is sinking each year, with the eastern side of the city sinking faster than the western side.

Over 400—the number of bridges that cross Venice's many waterways.

Under Water: Venice is prone to flooding, particularly in winter when the water level is at its highest. In 1966, floodwater reached a record-breaking 76 in (194 cm) deep.

THE ALGARVE

The Algarve is a region in southern Portugal that is known for its striking golden cliffs, sandy beaches, and almost year-round sunshine. The coastline is lapped by the Atlantic Ocean and is home to fascinating wildlife, such as dolphins, whales, and flocks of seabirds that soar above the waves.

Coastal Birds: Many types of seabird, such as shearwaters, petrels, and skuas, live around the coast and feed on fish, squid, and other marine creatures, which they pluck out of the water.

Sunshine and Sand: Portugal's sprawling southern coastline stretches for 96 miles (155 km) and is dotted with golden sandy beaches.

Hidden Caves: There are limestone caves and grottos to explore along the coastline, but many can only be reached by boat.

Feeding Ground: The water around the Algarve coastline is very nutritious and full of plankton, which dolphins, squid, and other sea creatures love to eat.

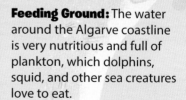

100—the number of beaches in the Algarve.

26—the number of cetacean (aquatic mammal) species, such as dolphins, porpoises, and whales, that live here.

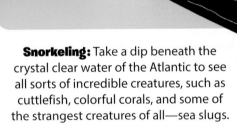

Acrobats: Dolphins are playful creatures that enjoy leaping out of the water, or breaching, and displaying aerial acrobatics.

Snorkeling: Take a dip beneath the crystal clear water of the Atlantic to see all sorts of incredible creatures, such as cuttlefish, colorful corals, and some of the strangest creatures of all—sea slugs.

200—the number of dolphins that may swim in a group, called a pod.

Bubble-blowing: Dolphins are very intelligent and have worked out how to herd their prey by blowing bubbles at them. They also swallow fish head first so that they don't get spiked by their fins!

MOSCOW

The capital of Russia and the largest city in Europe, Moscow is known for its colorful architecture. Its famous open space, Red Square, is home to many historic attractions.

Domes and Spires: St. Basil's Cathedral is an eye-catching church on Red Square. The building was finished in 1561 and is known for its decorative, onion-shaped domes.

Russian Dolls: A *matryoshka* (little matron) doll is a traditional painted wooden doll that twists open to reveal a smaller doll inside. Large dolls may have as many as 25 dolls hidden inside.

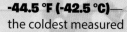

-44.5 °F (-42.5 °C)— the coldest measured temperature in Moscow, recorded during winter in 1940.

Red Square: Visitors flock to Moscow's best-known square to see its iconic sights. The most famous is probably the Kremlin, which is the center of Russian government as well as the official residence of the Russian president.

Bolshoi "Grand" Ballet: Built in 1766, the Bolshoi Theatre in Moscow is home to the oldest, and one of the most famous, ballet schools in the world.

Giant Fortress: Built in the 15th century, the Kremlin was originally a giant fortress. Today it is Moscow's most visited attraction, welcoming around 20 million visitors a year.

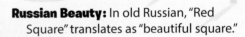

Russian Beauty: In old Russian, "Red Square" translates as "beautiful square."

In winter, ice rinks pop up all over the city and the parks are transformed into ski and sled runs. Even Red Square has its own ice-skating rink where people can go skating.

Africa

The second-largest continent after Asia, Africa straddles the Equator and experiences hot temperatures for most of the year. With sprawling deserts, giant waterfalls, dense rain forests, and tropical islands, Africa is full of extraordinary places to explore.

Marvel at the ancient pyramids of Egypt, hike deep into the forests of Rwanda to watch mountain gorillas play, or trek across the golden dunes of the Sahara, the world's largest desert. Venturing south, vast grasslands are home to prides of lions and herds of marching elephants, the world's biggest land animals. It is across these grassy plains that immense herds of wildebeest embark on an epic journey each year: The Great Migration.

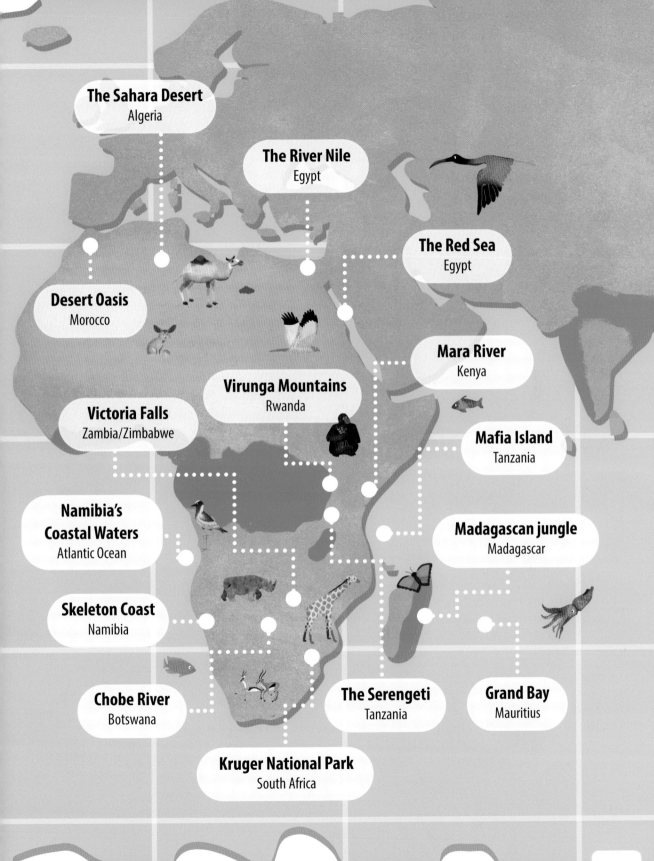

The Sahara Desert
Algeria

The River Nile
Egypt

The Red Sea
Egypt

Desert Oasis
Morocco

Mara River
Kenya

Virunga Mountains
Rwanda

Victoria Falls
Zambia/Zimbabwe

Mafia Island
Tanzania

Namibia's Coastal Waters
Atlantic Ocean

Madagascan jungle
Madagascar

Skeleton Coast
Namibia

Chobe River
Botswana

The Serengeti
Tanzania

Grand Bay
Mauritius

Kruger National Park
South Africa

THE SAHARA DESERT

Algeria is a North African country. Most of its people live near the northern coast which borders the Mediterranean Sea. Further inland is a large section of the Sahara desert, the world's largest hot desert. A huge expanse of sand and rock that stretches across North Africa, the Sahara is about the same size as the USA.

...... Gazelle

Surviving the Heat: Saharan animals have to cope with the hot, dry conditions. Gazelles have pale coats to reflect the Sun, jerboas live in underground burrows and camels can go for weeks without water.

...... Jerboa

Lizard

Creepy Crawlies: The desert is also home to ants, lizards, snakes, and dung beetles—these roll the poos of other animals into balls, where they lay their eggs.

Dung beetle

Algeria

100 °F (38 °C)—the temperature of the desert in the day, but temperatures can drop to near-freezing at night.

2.5 million—the number of nomadic (wandering) people living in the Sahara.

Ostrich

Sirocco Wind: Starting in the Sahara, the Sirocco is a hot, dry wind that blows dust across North Africa, sometimes reaching hurricane speeds.

Arid Algeria: Around 80 percent of Algeria is covered by the Sahara Desert.

Scrubland: Plants like shrubs and grasses grow roots that reach deep underground in search of buried water, but the driest parts of the desert are completely empty of plant life.

Bug Swarms: Locusts look similar to grasshoppers, but they can cause huge damage to crops and plants. Locusts move in giant swarms and can travel around 90 miles(150 km) in a day. Even a small swarm can eat the same amount of food as 35,000 people!

Horned viper

69

DESERT OASIS

Morocco is lapped by the Atlantic Ocean and the Mediterranean Sea. Farther inland, the Mediterranean landscape meets the sprawling Sahara Desert. Here, water is difficult to find and a spring called an oasis provides precious water for people and animals amid the hot sand dunes and rocky plains.

Scavengers: There are six species of vulture living in the Sahara Desert. Vultures feast on scraps of food that other creatures leave behind, like animal carcasses.

Fennec Fox: These desert foxes have ears that are 6 in (15 cm) in length. Their supersized ears help them to keep cool during the day and listen for prey at night.

Dorcas Gazelles: These horned animals are so well adapted to desert life that they don't even need to drink water. They get all the moisture they need from their food.

Super Stinger: The desert-living deathstalker scorpion is one of the most venomous species of scorpion in the world.

1,000 ft (300 m)—the height of the tallest sand dunes.

Camel Caravan: For thousands of years camels have carried people and goods, like tea, salt, cotton, and gold, across the desert wilderness. Up to 1,000 camels would walk in a long line called a "camel caravan."

Oasis: People and animals may travel for many miles to find a rare desert oasis. Desert palms and olive trees grow near these precious pools of water. There may even be the occasional crocodile!

THE RIVER NILE

Egypt is known for its many giant temples and pyramids. These were built thousands of years ago by a civilization that has long since vanished. Most are located on the banks of the River Nile, which runs north to south through the country. This is also where you'll find the capital, Cairo, one of Africa's largest cities.

11—the number of African countries that the River Nile flows through.

On the Water: People have been relying on the Nile for food and transport for thousands of years. All kinds of boats, from small fishing vessels to giant cruise ships, still use the river today.

4,100 miles (6,600 km)—the length of the River Nile, making it the longest river in the world.

Wafaa El-Nil: Every year, Egyptians celebrate the life-giving power of the Nile during a holiday called Wafaa El-Nil.

Growing Food: Crops like beans, flax, and wheat grow along the River Nile where the soil is full of nutrients from the river.

95 percent—the proportion of Egyptian people that live within a couple of miles of the River Nile.

The ancient Egyptians built many temples to their gods, including the double temple of Kom Ombo. Here, people could worship Sobek, the crocodile god, on one side and Horus, the falcon-headed god, on the other.

Over 2,000 years old— the age of the Kom Ombo Temple, with some parts thought to have been built around 187 BCE.

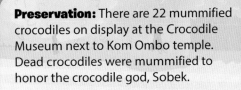

Preservation: There are 22 mummified crocodiles on display at the Crocodile Museum next to Kom Ombo temple. Dead crocodiles were mummified to honor the crocodile god, Sobek.

Flooding: In ancient times, the people living on the banks of the Nile relied on the yearly flood. This deposited nutrient-rich silt on the surrounding farmland, helping crops to grow.

Pyramids of Giza: Located just outside the city of Cairo, the Pyramids of Giza are giant limestone structures that were built more than 4,000 years ago as tombs for the ancient Egyptian kings. There are three main pyramids and the largest, the Great Pyramid, is around 460 ft (140 m) tall.

Over 3,000 years— the length of the Ancient Egyptian civilization, which lasted from 3100–30 BCE.

THE RED SEA

The Red Sea flows between the continents of Africa and Asia, stretching over 1,200 miles (2,000 km) from Suez in Egypt to the Gulf of Aden, where it meets the Arabian Sea. The Red Sea is one of the warmest and saltiest seas in the world with an abundance of colorful fish and sea creatures.

1,200—the number of fish species living in the Red Sea, and one in 10 of them are endemic (only found here).

·········· Lionfish

Over 200—the number of colorful coral species that grow in the Red Sea's crystal clear waters.

Ray ·····

Butterfly ······
fish

Red Blooms: The Red Sea gets its name from the giant blooms of red-brown algae that occasionally turn its waters a reddish-brown.

Angelfish

Green Turtles: These gentle creatures are one of the largest species of sea turtle. By grazing on plants, such as seagrass and algae, they help to keep the marine environment healthy. Green turtles migrate huge distances to lay their eggs, always returning to the beach where they hatched.

Lionfish: The stripy red-and-white body and long, spiky fins of a lionfish are a warning sign—these venomous fish can give a nasty sting.

Wrasse

Dugongs: Also known as sea cows, dugongs are mammals that swim in sheltered lagoons and warm water. The may live to be up to 70 years old.

THE SERENGETI

Tanzania, in the heart of East Africa, is known for its vast areas of wilderness. Grassy plains, dotted with rocky outcrops and flat-topped trees, stretch into the distance. Huge herds of wildlife feed and find shelter in the Serengeti National Park.

Grazing Animals: Across the grassy plains, cape buffalo, giraffes, gazelles, elephants, and wildebeest feed on the plentiful grass.

•••••• Wildebeest

Umbrella Trees: The grasslands are dotted with trees like the umbrella thorn acacia. This flat-topped tree has a wide canopy, giving it its name. Umbrella trees produce seeds in thick, spiral-shaped pods that curl around the tree's branches.

Keeping Watch: Big cats, such as cheetahs, lions, and caracals, stalk their prey, hiding in the long grass, ready to pounce.

50 mph (80 kph)—the speed that a Thompson's gazelle can run, making it one of the fastest land animals.

Rainy Seasons: The climate is usually warm and dry but rain arrives in March and again in October.

Balloon trips give visitors a birds-eye view of Africa's wild animals in their natural habitat.

12,000 sq miles (30,000 sq km)—the size of the Serengeti National Park.

1 million years—the length of time that the natural environment of the Serengeti has remained unchanged.

6.8 tons (7,000 kg)—the weight of an African elephant, making it the world's largest land animal.

20 in (50 cm)—the length of a giraffe's tongue, which it uses to hook onto branches and pull leaves into its mouth.

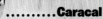..........Caracal

MARA RIVER

When the dry season arrives in the Serengeti, herds of wildebeest migrate north in search of food. This epic journey, known as the Great Migration, spans two countries—Tanzania and Kenya. The journey is perilous, particularly when the herds have to cross rivers where crocodiles are ready to pounce.

1.5 million—the number of wildebeest that embark on the long journey across the grasslands.

Nile Crocodiles: Thousands of hungry crocodiles lie in wait for wildebeest when they dare cross the water.

Kings of the Savanna: Lions are fierce hunters and top of the Serengeti food chain. They are sociable animals and choose to live together in large groups called prides. When not on the hunt, lions can be found napping under trees—often for around 18 hours each day!

After the birth of their calves in March, wildebeest begin migrating north in search of food. They will return after the next rainy season in November, when there is grass to eat again.

Speedy Cats: Cheetahs are the fastest land animals in the world. They can sprint at speeds of up to 80 mph (130 km/h) when chasing down prey.

600 miles (1,000 km)—the distance that animals travel during the Great Migration.

Giant Herds: Hundreds of thousands of zebras and gazelles travel alongside the wildebeest.

500,000—the number of wildebeest calves that are born in spring each year in the Serengeti.

MAFIA ISLAND

Located off the coast of East Africa, Mafia Island is a tropical paradise of white-sand beaches lapped by the Indian Ocean. Shimmering fish dart through clear blue waters and giant whale sharks swim in the deep.

Marine Park: Mafia Island Marine Park was set up in 1995 to protect the precious ocean habitats around the island, as well as the amazing creatures that live there.

.... Seagull

400—the number of fish species around Mafia island, including bright clownfish, slinky octopuses, gliding rays, dolphins, and sharks.

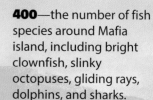

60 cm (24 in)—the size of a baby whale shark when it is born, but it will grow to be the largest fish in the ocean!

40 ft (12 m)—the size of an adult whale shark; that's around the same length as a bus!

Conservation Projects:
Whale sharks are an endangered species and people are working hard to protect them. Individual sharks can be identified by their unique patterns of spots, so researchers are able to track individual sharks to learn more about them.

Spice Island: Mafia Island is known for the rich variety of spices that it produces, including cinnamon, cloves, nutmeg, and black pepper.

Growing Old: Whale sharks can live to be up to 70 years old. Most whale sharks stay close to the island throughout their lives.

Squid . . . .

VIRUNGA MOUNTAINS

Rwanda is a small country in the east of Africa. One of the largest populations of mountain gorillas lives here in the rich green forests of the Virunga Mountains. This chain of extinct volcanoes spans the borders of Rwanda, Uganda, and the Democratic Republic of Congo.

1,000—the number of mountain gorillas living in the wild in Africa.

The High Life: Mountain gorillas live at high altitudes up to 13,000 ft (4,000 m) above sea level.

Nose Print: A gorilla can be recognized by the unique shape and size of its leathery nose!

98 percent—the amount of DNA that we, as humans, share with gorillas.

It gets bitterly cold in the mountains, so mountain gorillas have a thick coat of fur to keep them warm when the temperature drops and the forest is blanketed in mist.

14,788 ft (4,507 m)—the height of the tallest dormant volcano in Rwanda's Volcanoes National Park.

Jungle Snakes: Africa is home to some of the most incredible and dangerous snakes in the animal kingdom, and they come in all colors and sizes. The black mamba is feared for its lightning fast strike and the gaboon viper has the longest fangs of any venomous snake.

Safe Place: Around 12 families of mountain gorillas are protected inside Rwanda's Volcanoes National Park.

Troop: A group of gorillas is called a troop. At least one silverback (dominant male), several females, and their young live in a troop.

Silverback: The whitish hair on the back of a dominant adult male gorilla marks him out as the leader of a group.

83

VICTORIA FALLS

Located on the border between Zambia and Zimbabwe, Victoria Falls is one of the world's largest waterfalls. Here, water tumbles down deep chasms cut into the rock. Elephants, buffalo, and the occasional lion can be spotted in the national parks around the falls.

Victoria Falls is roughly twice the height of Niagara Falls in the USA.

Giant Curtain: At over 1 m (1.7 km) wide at the point where the Zambezi River tumbles over its rocky plateau, the falls creates the biggest curtain of water in the world.

..... **Bee-eater**

Nesting Place: The river and falls provide habitats for many different birds, including ibis and bee-eaters. Birds of prey, like eagles and falcons, soar above the crashing water and nest in the cliffs around the falls.

354 ft (108 m)—the height of Victoria Falls, creating a tall sheet of crashing water.

Moonbow: On a full moon, you may spot a lunar rainbow as moonlight shines through water from the falls. This rare sight can only be seen in a few places on Earth.

Ibis

Bungee Jumping: If they dare, visitors can bungee jump off a bridge next to the falls, free-falling an exhilarating 364 ft (111 m) toward the Zambezi River below.

12 miles (20 km)— how far away the tumbling clouds of white mist can be seen, giving the falls the local name "the smoke that thunders."

Hippopotamus: Despite their cumbersome size, hippos are surprisingly good swimmers. They live in the Zambezi River and spend around 16 hours each day bathing to keep cool. Hippos can hold their breath for up to five minutes!

Boat Trips: One of the best ways to see Victoria Falls is by taking a boat along the Zambezi River. That way, you can feel the spray of water from the falls.

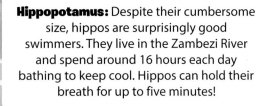

SKELETON COAST

In Namibia, in southwest Africa, the mighty Namib desert meets the sea, creating a long sandy coastline. But these are no ordinary beaches. Rough seas and thick fog have seen hundreds of ships wrecked here. Their remains stick out of the sand like bones, giving the region its name: the Skeleton Coast.

500—the number of shipwrecks that lie stranded along the coastline, with many hidden beneath the sea or sand.

300 miles (500 km)—the length of the Skeleton Coast, made up of barren beaches and dunes that stretch 25 miles (40 km) inland.

Changing Coastline:
In 1909, a ship called *Eduard Bohlen* was stranded on the Skeleton Coast. The shape of the coastline has changed so much that the shipwreck is now 0.6 miles (1 km) inland!

Thirst Quencher: Any plant that survives here has to rely on the daily fog rolling in for water.

300 ft (100 m)—the height of the golden sand dunes before they plunge into the Atlantic Sea.

At the coastline, there is nothing but sea and sand for hundreds of miles around (apart from shipwrecks). Sailors shipwrecked here were a long way from help.

Manure Mishap: A ship called *Otavi* was shipwrecked on the Skeleton Coast in 1945, along with its cargo of guano—a fertilizer made from seabird poop!

Desert Lions: Namibia is home to rare desert lions that have adapted to the harsh environment by preying on the abundant fur seals.

Fur Seals: Over 100,000 fur seals live in a single colony on the Skeleton Coast, and all are competing for food and space—it's a noisy, smelly place. Fur seals are strong swimmers. They can dive to 660 ft (200 m) and hold their breath for up to 7.5 minutes.

NAMIBIA'S COASTAL WATERS

With so many shipwrecks along the west coast of Africa, it's the perfect place to go hunting for lost treasure dropped by sunken ships. Namibia has one of the longest coastlines on the west coast of Africa—providing plenty of diving spots for treasure-seekers.

Hammerhead shark

Trade Routes: In the 1600s, ships began sailing between Europe and Asia as people started buying and selling products around the world. This hazardous journey took sailors all the way around the coast of Africa, where ships were at the mercy of violent storms and pirate attacks!

Treasure Troves: Trade ships were laden with silk, spices, cotton, and tea to sell back home, as well as gold and silver coins.

Finding Shelter: Shipwrecks are broken down by buffeting currents. Over time, sea anemones, coral, and fish begin to make their homes in nooks and crannies. These creatures attract predators such as hammer-head sharks, which hunt for prey in the wreckage.

Diving for Shipwrecks: The best way to explore a shipwreck is by diving down to have a look. Wreck diving is a popular activity around the world as there is so much history to discover and wildlife to spot.

Around 40–80 crew members lived on board trade ships for around six months at a time. Without access to fresh food or clean water, life on board was tough.

Treasure Haul: One of the oldest and most valuable shipwrecks ever discovered was found off the west coast of Africa. The shipwreck had been a Portuguese ship that set sail in 1533. Around 44,000 copper ingots were discovered at the shipwreck along with many rare Portuguese coins.

CHOBE RIVER

Botswana is a landlocked country at the heart of southern Africa. Snaking through the landscape of Botswana, the Chobe River attracts huge herds of elephants, hippos, and wildebeest that come to drink and bathe.

Around 70 percent of Botswana is covered by the Kalahari Desert.

Room to Grow: A baby elephant is just 3 ft (1 m) tall when it is born, but it will grow to be over 10 ft (3 m) tall.

130,000—the number of African elephants living in Botswana, the biggest population of African elephants in the world.

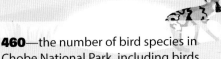

460—the number of bird species in Chobe National Park, including birds of prey, vultures, waterbirds, and seasonal migrating birds.

African Wild Dogs: These "painted" wolf-like dogs travel up to 30 miles (50 km) each day to find food. They are social creatures, hunting together in packs of up to 20 dogs. They also share their food and care for their pups as a group.

40,000—the number of muscles in an elephant's trunk, helping it drink, grab food, and make its trumpet call.

Up to 100 years—the lifespan of the Nile crocodile, which feeds on fish and any larger prey it can get its teeth into.

Animals come from far and wide to bathe in and drink from the deep blue Chobe River, which cuts through the desert landscape.

KRUGER NATIONAL PARK

On the pointed southernmost tip of the African continent is the country of South Africa. There are 20 national parks in South Africa, each giving visitors the chance to get close to amazing animals in their natural habitats. Kruger National Park is one of the largest national parks in the world.

Hyena

Sable antelope

Greater kudu

Malachite sunbird

3,000 Year-Old-Trees: Native baobab trees can be seen across Africa and some are thousands of years old!

7,700 sq miles (20,000 sq km)— the size of the Kruger National Park, stretching 220 miles (350 km) from north to south.

...... Vervet monkey

...... Masked weaver bird

The Watering Hole: During the dry season, animals come from miles around to quench their thirst at the watering hole.

Sharing Water: Big creatures such as hippos, lions, and zebras drink alongside smaller animals like hyenas, sable antelope, ostriches, greater kudus, baboons, and vervet monkeys. Weaver birds, sunbirds, swallows, and hoopoes swoop down to the water from nearby trees.

..... Barn
swallow

4x4 safari vehicles rumble along the bumpy terrain letting visitors get right up close to incredible wildlife.

18 ft (5.5 m)—the height of a giraffe, making it the tallest living land animal.

On Guard: The towering height and sharp vision of a giraffe helps it to keep a lookout for predators, like prowling lions and hyenas.

Baboon ....

Wildlife Giants: Elephants, lions, rhinos, leopards, and buffalo can be spotted during safari tours.

.... Hoopoe

Swimming with Sharks: The South African coast is home to the largest predatory fish in the world—the great white shark. These giant creatures grow to 15 ft (4.6 m) long! They have sharp, ragged teeth and a bloodthirsty appetite, yet people choose to dive with them, protected by a strong metal cage.

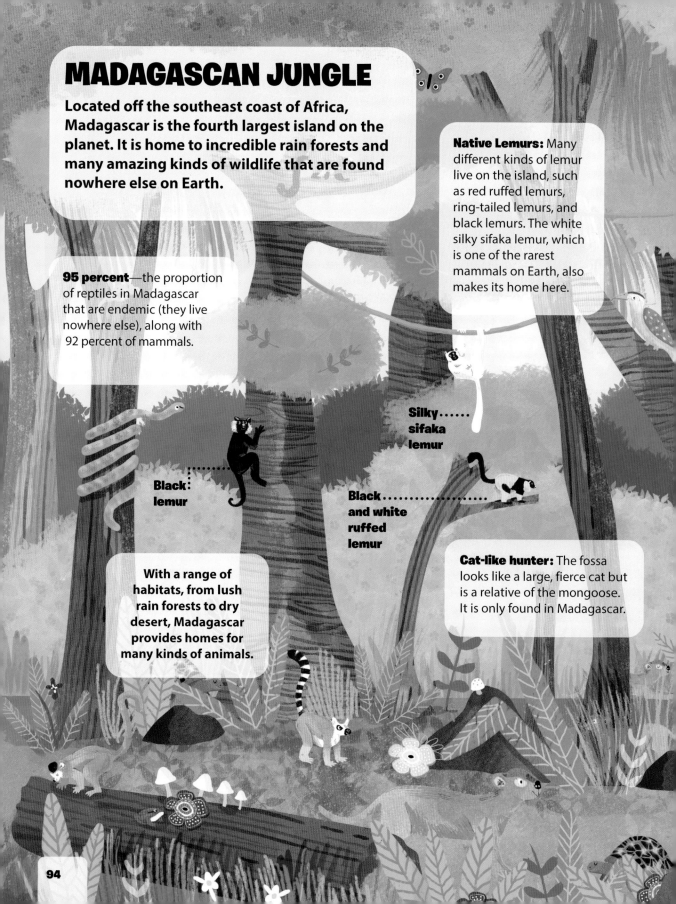

MADAGASCAN JUNGLE

Located off the southeast coast of Africa, Madagascar is the fourth largest island on the planet. It is home to incredible rain forests and many amazing kinds of wildlife that are found nowhere else on Earth.

Native Lemurs: Many different kinds of lemur live on the island, such as red ruffed lemurs, ring-tailed lemurs, and black lemurs. The white silky sifaka lemur, which is one of the rarest mammals on Earth, also makes its home here.

95 percent—the proportion of reptiles in Madagascar that are endemic (they live nowhere else), along with 92 percent of mammals.

Silky ...... sifaka lemur

Black lemur

Black .... and white ruffed lemur

With a range of habitats, from lush rain forests to dry desert, Madagascar provides homes for many kinds of animals.

Cat-like hunter: The fossa looks like a large, fierce cat but is a relative of the mongoose. It is only found in Madagascar.

Butterfly Kingdom: Giant butterflies flit from flower to flower, collecting nectar to eat—around 300 different species of them! The Madagascar giant swallowtail has an incredible 5.5-in- (14-cm-) wide wingspan and is one of over 200 butterflies that are endemic.

70–90 percent— the proportion of wildlife that lives up in the trees, above the shaded forest floor.

Madagascar giant swallowtail

Ring-tailed lemur

Red ruffed Lemur

11,000—the number of endemic plant species that only grow in Madagascar.

615—the number of newly discovered species in Madagascar, measured over a ten-year period.

Fossa

GRAND BAY

Mauritius is around 1,200 miles (2,000 km) off the southeast coast of Africa, surrounded by the Indian Ocean. In the north of the island is a small fishing village called Grand Bay. When the weather is warmest, between November and April, huge storms called cyclones bring high winds and torrential rain to the beaches here.

Land of Volcanoes: Mauritius and its nearby islands are part of a chain of volcanic islands that were formed around 10 million years ago.

110 miles (175 km)—the length of the coastline of Mauritius, with miles of silver-white sandy beaches.

Up to five—the number of cyclones that sweep past Mauritius every year, causing strong winds, rain, and rough seas.

Tuna

Marlin

Tropical coconut palms grow all over the island and coconuts are used in many traditional recipes, like creamy curries and coconut sweets.

Talipot Palm: Growing up to 80 ft (25 m) tall, the talipot palm is one of the largest palm trees in the world. It only flowers once in its life, sometimes bursting into several million small flowers. Usually this happens when the talipot is between 30 and 80 years old!

Tropical Wildlife: Beautiful coral reefs surround the island, forming shallow clear lagoons which are home to around 400 species of sea creature.

Deep-sea Divers: Humpback whales, sperm whales, bottlenose dolphins, tropical fish, and deep-sea fish, like tuna and marlin, can be spotted around the island—but they stay hidden deep beneath the waves when cyclones hit.

Asia

Asia is the largest continent on Earth, stretching from the frozen Arctic all the way to the Equator. With majestic mountain ranges, ancient desert civilizations, and record-breaking buildings, there are countless amazing places to explore.

On a trip to Asia, you could find yourself battling snowstorms in the Himalayas or trekking across the hot, dry deserts of Uzbekistan—this is a land of extremes! Marvel at the view atop the world's tallest building in Dubai, or camp out under the stars in the Arabian desert. Venture deep into the Malaysian jungle to watch orangutans in their natural habitat, or jump on board a submersible in the Pacific Ocean to explore the deepest underwater trench on Earth.

Baikonur Cosmodrome
Kazakhstan

Gobi Desert
Mongolia

Kyzylkum Desert
Uzbekistan

Mount Everest
Nepal/Tibet

Hong Kong
China

Tokyo
Japan

Darjeeling Railway
India

Wadi Rum
Jordan

Bangkok
Thailand

Delhi
India

Dhaka
Bangladesh

Dubai
United Arab Emirates

Malaysian Jungle
Malaysia

The Mariana Trench
Pacific Ocean

WADI RUM

In southern Jordan, on the edge of the Arabian Desert, is Wadi Rum—a giant desert canyon where Bedouin people have made their homes for thousands of years. Here, Bedouin camps welcome visitors and provide a glimpse of traditional Bedouin customs and ways of life.

Worlds Away: With its endless red-orange sand and craggy sandstone mountains, Wadi Rum is also known as "Valley of the Moon."

280 sq miles (725 sq km)—the size of Wadi Rum, making it the largest valley in Jordan and about the same size as New York City.

Dressed for the Heat: Traditional Arabian clothing includes a long white robe called a *dishdasha* and a white or checked headdress that protects the wearer from the sun.

Tea Time: Authentic Bedouin tea is brewed with herbs, such as sage, mint, and thyme, which are found growing in the desert. Often spices are added, along with sugar.

Traditional Food: Meals are cooked over a fire—or even underground! *Zarb* is a meal of meat, rice, and vegetables roasted for 24 hours on hot coals under the sand. The name means "to hide" in Arabic.

12,000—the number of years that Bedouin people are thought to have lived in the desert, camping with their animals and moving frequently to find food and water.

Bedouin Coffee: Welcoming guests is an important tradition in Bedouin culture. Visitors are offered three cups of coffee on arrival and each has a meaning—the first is to honor the guest, the second celebrates bravery, and the third blesses the party with a good mood.

Changing Climate: Ancient cave drawings show that the desert may have been very different thousands of years ago, with vineyards and olive groves growing, and animals like lions and ostriches living here.

Camel Caravan: Chains of camels, called camel caravans, have been transporting people and heavy loads across the desert for thousands of years—and still do today.

In the summer, the temperature can soar to a scorching 118 °F (48 °C) and sandstorms whip up huge clouds of sand.

DUBAI

Dubai is a sprawling desert city on the coast of the United Arab Emirates. In just a few decades, the city has grown from a small fishing village into a skyscraper-packed city. People travel here from all over the world to see Dubai's modern attractions. These include record-breaking buildings and the Dubai Mall, one of the largest shopping centers on Earth.

Supersized: The Dubai Mall is so big that it has its own aquarium. Here, visitors can explore rain forest, shoreline, and ocean habitats, and discover the amazing creatures that live there.

2,200,000 gallons (10,000,000 liters)— the amount of water that the aquarium tank holds, providing a home to 400 species of sharks and rays and around 33,000 animals in total.

Burj Khalifa: At a whopping 2,717 ft (828 m) tall, the Burj Khalifa is the tallest building in the world and can be seen from almost anywhere in Dubai. It has 160 stories and a super-high-speed elevator which carries visitors up to the highest observation deck ever built.

1,200—the number of shops in the Dubai Mall, containing everything from high-end gadgets, to designer clothes and luxury gifts.

80 million—the number of people that visit the Dubai Mall every year, making it the most popular shopping center in the world.

Shoes

Toy SHOP

Getting Crowded:
Each year, the Dubai Mall has more tourists visiting from around the world than New York City!

Endless Entertainment:
There's a lot more to do than shopping. Visitors can go ice skating, trampolining, to the cinema, or even play games in the virtual reality park.

Escaping the Heat:
During the summer, temperatures can reach a scorching 104 °F (40 °C), but air conditioning keeps the Dubai Mall nice and cool.

BAIKONUR COSMODROME

Kazakhstan is a vast country with no coastline, bordered by Russia to the north and China to the east. Within Kazakhstan's sparse grasslands is the Baikonur Cosmodrome. This record-breaking space center is the launch site for a type of Russian spacecraft called Soyuz, which is the most-used launch vehicle in the world.

1957—the year that the first man-made satellite, *Sputnik 1*, was launched into space from the Baikonur Cosmodrome.

Top Secret: The space center's name is misleading as Baikonur was originally the name of a small mining town over 200 miles (320 km) away from the launch site. This was done on purpose to keep the true location a secret.

Russian Property: Despite its location in Kazakhstan, the Cosmodrome and its flights are operated by Russia. It leases the land from Kazakhstan.

Space Dog: The first animal to orbit Earth was Laika, a stray dog from the streets of Moscow. Laika was launched into outer-orbit from the Baikonur Cosmodrome in 1957, on board a spacecraft called *Sputnik 2*.

Extreme Temperatures: The cosmodrome is set in a remote landscape where temperatures can range from -40 °F (-40 °C) in winter to 104 °F (40 °C) in summer.

Docking in Space: The tip of the spacecraft carries the tools needed to dock with the International Space Station, which is 250 miles (400 km) above Earth.

World First: In 1961, Yuri Gagarin became the first human to go into space. He was launched from the Baikonur Cosmodrome aboard the spacecraft *Vostok 1*.

1,680—the number of successful rocket launches in a Russian Soyuz rocket since 1957.

Each Russian Soyuz spacecraft measures 24 ft (7.2 m) in length, 9 ft (2.7 m) in diameter, and weighs 7.7 tons (7 tonnes).

Three—the number of astronauts that can fit inside a Soyuz space vehicle.

KYZYLKUM DESERT

Stretching across Uzbekistan and parts of Kazakhstan in Central Asia, the Kyzylkum Desert is the fifth-largest desert on the continent. Here, people go camel trekking across vast sloping dunes and stay in traditional camps amid miles of open sand.

"Kyzylkum" translates as "red sand" in Turkic languages.

115,000 sq miles (300,000 sq km)— the size of the Kyzylkum Desert, making it the 15th largest in the world.

Precious Water: Desert camps are built near oases, where people and livestock can find vital water to drink.

Ancient Civilizations: People have been living in the desert since 2100 BCE, moving around to find water, and raising livestock like goats for milk, meat, and wool.

Mountain Ranges: Rising above the desert sands, mountain caves provide homes for gerbils and hopping rodents called jerboas. At night, small wild cats, called sand cats, emerge from dens to hunt for small mammals.

Bactrian Camel: A thirsty Bactrian camel can drink up to a quarter of its body weight in one go! Fat reserves are stored in the two humps on its back, allowing camels to travel huge distances without stopping to eat. Unlike Arabian camels, Bactrian camels have a thick, shaggy coat to protect them in winter, when temperatures can drop below freezing.

Shelter: Traditional Circular tents called yurts are made using camel hair, providing a cosy place for weary travelers to sleep.

Scrubland: Low, prickly bushes are home to ground squirrels, hares, and tortoises.

Desert Food: Homemade bread, camel milk, and meat from local livestock are some of the traditional foods eaten in the desert.

Desert Blooms: In spring, the desert unexpectedly bursts into life with colorful poppies, blossoms, and lilac flowers.

Sand cat ......

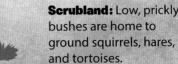

Gerbil ....

107

MOUNT EVEREST

On the border between Nepal and Tibet in China, in the midst of the snow-capped Himalayan mountains, is the highest point on Earth: Mount Everest. Capped by snow and ice and buffeted by treacherous weather, the mountain offers a death-defying challenge for the most daring mountaineers.

Mount Everest base camp →

29,032 ft (8,849 m)— the height of Mount Everest, making it the tallest mountain above sea level.

Growing Taller: Mount Everest is 50 to 60 million years old and still growing! The rocks that make up Earth's crust are pushing the mountain higher by about 0.2 in (0.5 cm) each year.

Local Knowledge: Experienced guides prepare the route with ropes and ladders to make the journey safer, but it's still a difficult and dangerous climb.

The top of Mount Everest is around the same height as passenger planes fly—imagine that view!

Snow Dome: The very top of Mount Everest is a small mound of snow that is about the same size as a dining room table. Around six people can stand on top of it at one time.

Death Zone: Once you climb above 26,000 ft (8,000 m) there is very little oxygen to breathe and climbers can suffer from altitude sickness. This is called the "death zone."

1953—the year that Tenzing Norgay from Nepal and Edmund Hillary from New Zealand became the first mountaineers to reach the summit of Mount Everest.

Base Camp: Before attempting the strenuous five-day trek to the summit, climbers rest at one of two Everest base camps, on either the Nepalese or the Chinese side of the mountain. Here, climbers stock up on food and equipment, and get used to the high altitude.

One in 100—the chance of dying while climbing Mount Everest, yet hundreds of mountaineers attempt to reach the summit every year.

DARJEELING RAILWAY

In the foothills of the Himalayan mountains in northeast India, antique steam engines chug along steep winding tracks. Passing stunning mountain scenery and green tea plantations, the route carries passengers between New Jalpaiguri and the hill town of Darjeeling.

1881—the year that the Darjeeling Himalayan Railway (DHR) began ferrying passengers up and down the mountainous terrain.

Red panda

Toy Train: With narrow tracks that are just 2 ft (0.6 m) wide and trains with tiny engines, it's no wonder that the Darjeeling Himalayan Railway has been nicknamed the "Toy Train."

6,900 ft (2,100 m)—how high the DHR climbs as it makes its winding journey from New Jalpaiguri to Darjeeling.

Snow Leopard: These big cats roam far and wide across the Himalayan mountains. They like to keep themselves hidden and are the only big cats that can't roar! Snow leopards are at home in craggy mountain slopes and can leap up to 50 ft (15 m) from ledge to ledge.

28,169 ft (8,586 m)—the height of Kanchenjunga mountain, seen here, which is the third-tallest mountain in the world.

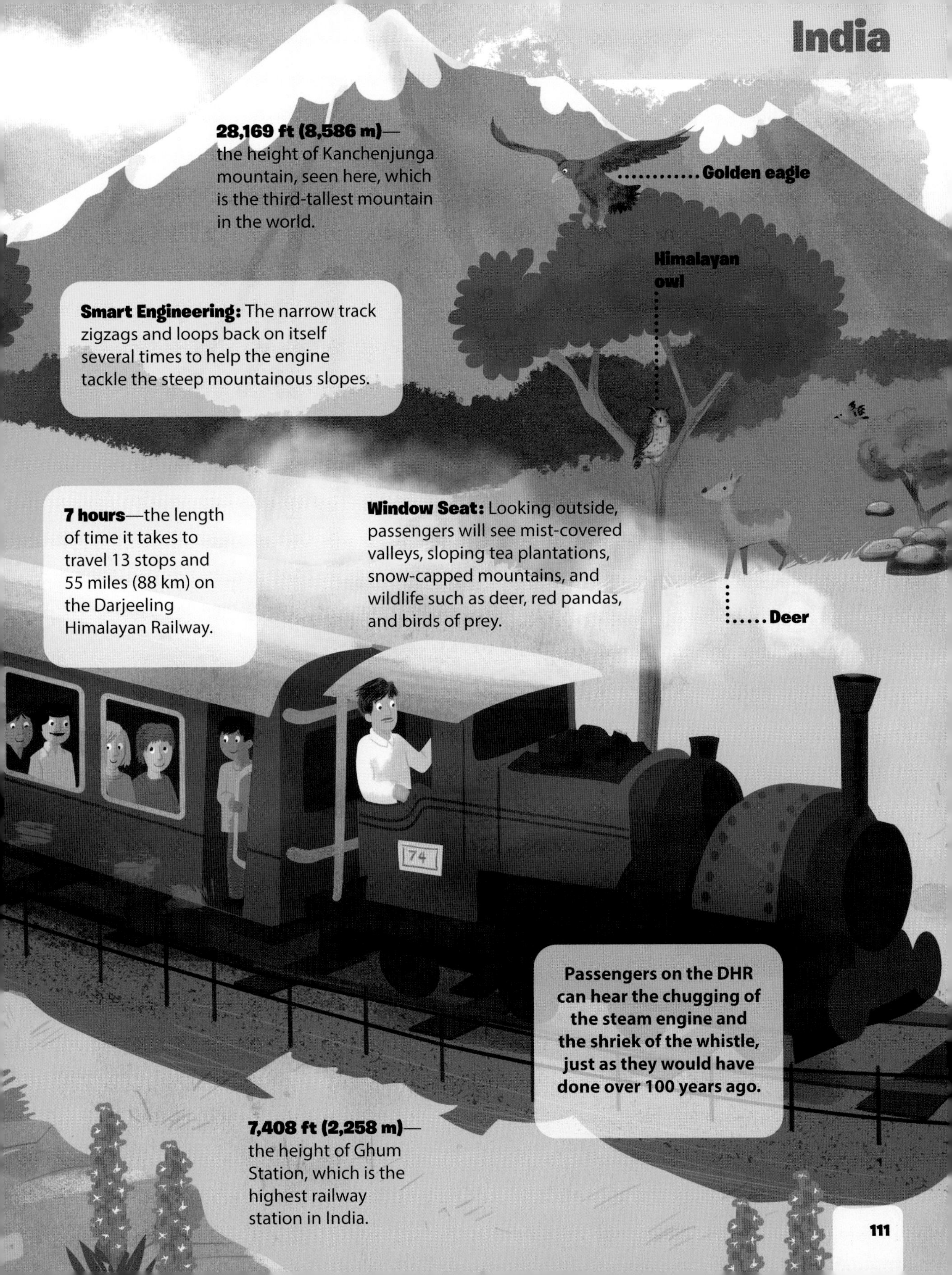

············ **Golden eagle**

Himalayan owl

Smart Engineering: The narrow track zigzags and loops back on itself several times to help the engine tackle the steep mountainous slopes.

7 hours—the length of time it takes to travel 13 stops and 55 miles (88 km) on the Darjeeling Himalayan Railway.

Window Seat: Looking outside, passengers will see mist-covered valleys, sloping tea plantations, snow-capped mountains, and wildlife such as deer, red pandas, and birds of prey.

······ **Deer**

74

Passengers on the DHR can hear the chugging of the steam engine and the shriek of the whistle, just as they would have done over 100 years ago.

7,408 ft (2,258 m)—the height of Ghum Station, which is the highest railway station in India.

DELHI

Delhi, the capital city of India, is packed with ancient temples, magical forts, modern shops, and bustling traditional markets. At the heart of Old Delhi is a sprawling outdoor market called Chandni Chowk where shoppers can find anything from spices and clothes to electronic gadgets.

Food Stalls: Bustling street food stalls cook mountains of sizzling, steaming hot snacks for hungry shoppers.

Indian Dance: Bangra is an energetic style of music and dancing that is often performed at parties and special occasions.

Chole Bhature: A popular street-food snack in Delhi is a plate of fragrant chickpea curry served with deep-fried dough.

1650—the date that Delhi's largest spice market opened, selling pungent local herbs and spices in a dazzling array of colors.

On the Loose: Stray cows wander freely on many streets in India, narrowly missed by tooting rickshaws and clattering wooden carts. Cows are sacred animals according to the Hindu religion and are treated with great respect.

Winding Streets: Tiny shops overflowing with sparkling jewelry, colorful fabrics, electronics, and things to eat line the market's narrow lanes.

Indian Elephants: Many people in India believe that the elephant is a sacred animal and so elephants get pampered and fed their favorite foods, like bananas. An Indian elephant can spend up to 19 hours each day eating!

People come from across the city to buy fabrics, lace, jewelry, tinsel, and colorful decorations for parties and ceremonies.

The Taj Mahal: In the city of Agra in northern India is the gleaming Taj Mahal. This ancient tomb was completed in 1653—it took 20 years to build and around 1,000 elephants helped by transporting heavy materials. The tomb is made from white marble and set with precious jewels from across Asia, like jade and turquoise.

DHAKA

The capital city of Bangladesh, Dhaka is a noisy, chaotic, and fascinating place. Away from the city, the countryside of Bangladesh is rich and green, but here in Dhaka, thousands of rickshaws and millions of people compete for space in one of the busiest cities in the world.

City Roots: Dhaka was founded in 1610 and quickly became a bustling place of trade.

The most popular way to navigate the busy streets of Dhaka is on a three-wheeled bike called a rickshaw.

500,000—the number of rickshaws that are thought to be rattling around the roads of Dhaka.

21 million—the number of people living in the city of Dhaka, making it one of the top 10 most populated cities in the world.

Bengal Tiger: Living in the forests of Bangladesh, Bengal tigers are celebrated as the country's national animal. Each tiger has a unique pattern of orange and black stripes—no two are exactly the same. In the wild, these fierce hunters will travel many miles while hunting at night and their roar can be heard up to 2 miles (3 km) away!

Six Seasons: As well as spring, summer, autumn, and winter, Bangladesh has a rainy season and a cool season.

Islamic Heritage: Also known as the "City of Mosques," Dhaka has around 1,000 Islamic places of worship.

BANGKOK

With majestic palaces, ornate temples, and traditional markets where you can buy fresh food and local delicacies, Thailand's capital city is full of extraordinary places to explore. For over 100 years, Bangkok's floating markets have been a way of life for local people and are packed full of fascinating things to see.

Early Birds: As the sun rises in Bangkok, floating markets come to life with shoppers seeking the freshest local fruits, vegetables, herbs, and spices.

Staple Foods: In Thailand, rice is eaten with most meals. Millions of tons are grown here every year.

Herbs and Spices: Thai cooking is packed with flavor from ingredients like chillis, garlic, peppers, and lemon grass, and fish sauce adds a potent fishy tang.

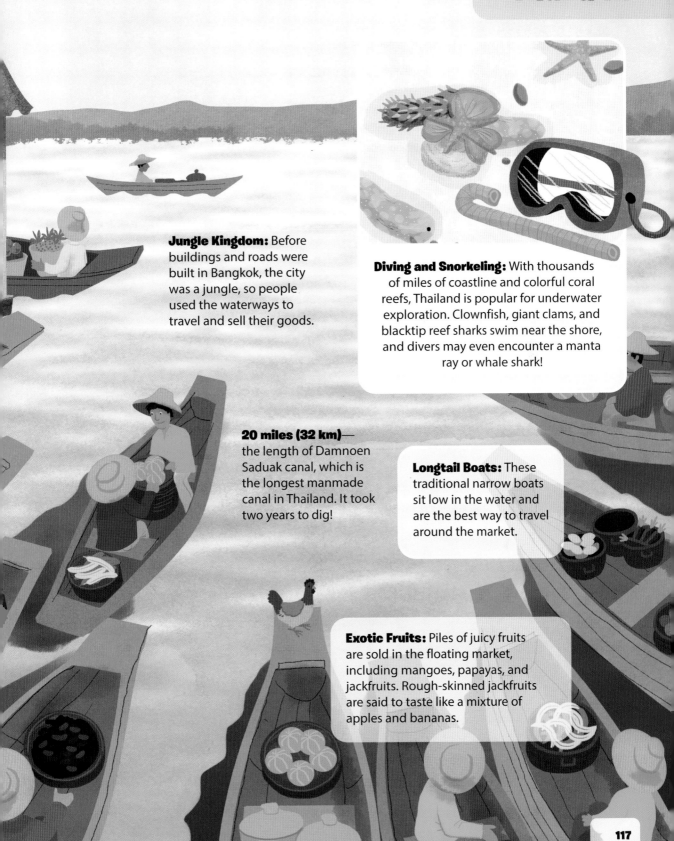

Jungle Kingdom: Before buildings and roads were built in Bangkok, the city was a jungle, so people used the waterways to travel and sell their goods.

Diving and Snorkeling: With thousands of miles of coastline and colorful coral reefs, Thailand is popular for underwater exploration. Clownfish, giant clams, and blacktip reef sharks swim near the shore, and divers may even encounter a manta ray or whale shark!

20 miles (32 km)— the length of Damnoen Saduak canal, which is the longest manmade canal in Thailand. It took two years to dig!

Longtail Boats: These traditional narrow boats sit low in the water and are the best way to travel around the market.

Exotic Fruits: Piles of juicy fruits are sold in the floating market, including mangoes, papayas, and jackfruits. Rough-skinned jackfruits are said to taste like a mixture of apples and bananas.

MALAYSIAN JUNGLE

As the sun rises in Danum Valley Conservation Area in Malaysia, the dense green rain forest comes alive with the sights and sounds of nature. Here, endangered orangutans forage in the treetops and hundreds of species of birds flit between branches.

Malaysian blue spider

Living in Safety: The Danum Valley Conservation Area stretches for 170 sq miles (440 sq km). This protected area is one of the world's best places to see orangutans in the wild.

People of the Forest: Orangutans are large apes with shaggy red fur that live in the rain forests of Malaysia and Indonesia. In the local languages, "orangutan" means "person of the forest."

Praying mantis

500—the number of Bornean orangutans left in the Danum Valley, making them an endangered species.

130 million years—the age of the Danum Valley rain forest, which is home to a dazzling array of wildlife with no people to disturb it.

Swing Time: An orangutan's long, strong arms help it to climb and swing from tree to tree across the rain forest canopy.

Creepy Crawlies: Hiding in the leaves and crawling up tree trunks are all kinds of insects, from Malaysian blue spiders and lantern bugs to giant millipedes and praying mantises.

Durian Fruit: These strange, spiky, and very smelly fruits grow across Malaysia and are a common snack—although they're not to everyone's taste. In fact, they smell so strong they have been banned from many types of public transport in Southeast Asia!

Giant millipede ....

Fruity Feast: Orangutans forage for fruits like sweet lychees and plump figs that grow in the rain forest trees.

.... Lantern bug

GOBI DESERT

The Gobi Desert stretches around 1,000 miles (1,600 km) across large parts of Mongolia and China in eastern Asia. Around 80 million years ago, dinosaurs roamed the land, and their fossils can still be found today. Here, we go beneath the desert's rocky surface and into its fossil beds to discover the amazing creatures that lived here millions of years ago.

In the Mongolian language, "gobi" means "waterless place."

Citipati: This giant, bird-like dinosaur was nearly 10 ft (3 m) long! It was found on top of a nest of fossilized eggs.

Modern Mammals: Instead of dinosaurs, wild camels, gazelles and many kinds of rodents live in the Gobi Desert today.

Giant Lizard: Estesia was around 8 ft (2.4 m) in length and is closely related to large lizards alive today. Although, unlike most modern lizards, Estesia is thought to have had a venomous bite.

80 million years—the age of the first ever dinosaur eggs to be found, discovered in the Gobi Desert in the 1920s.

Velociraptor: This dinosaur lived around 80 million years ago and had talons like an eagle.

Ukhaatherium: It wasn't just dinosaurs living here around 80 million years ago. Small early mammals like Ukhaatherium also lived alongside them.

Mongolian Gers: A traditional Mongolian home in the desert is called a "ger," which means "home." Gers are made from natural materials found in the desert, like camel wool. Mongolian people living in the desert are often nomadic and move around with their animals. Their round, tent-like homes are quick to put up and take down to help people move more easily.

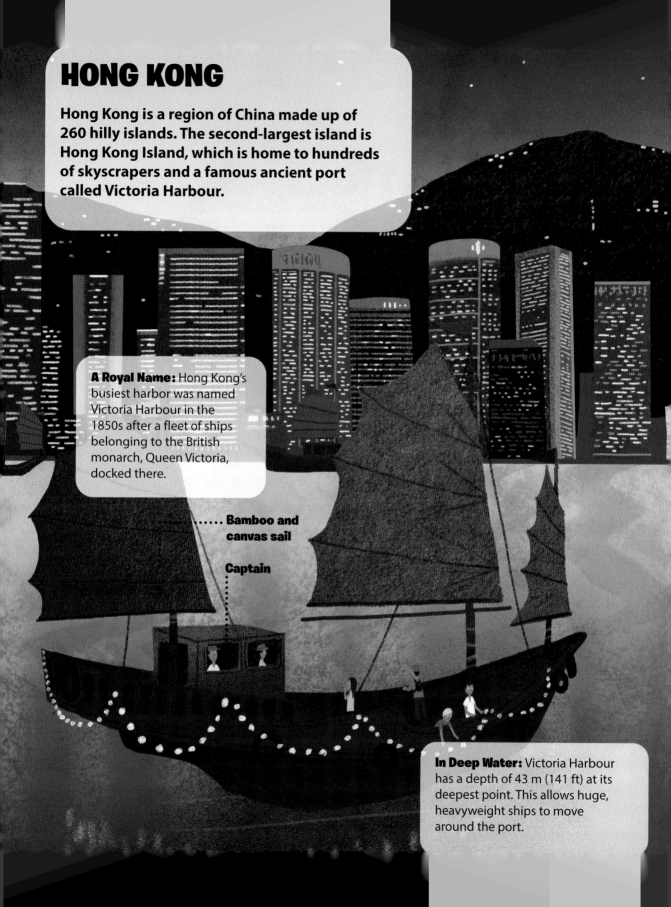

HONG KONG

Hong Kong is a region of China made up of 260 hilly islands. The second-largest island is Hong Kong Island, which is home to hundreds of skyscrapers and a famous ancient port called Victoria Harbour.

A Royal Name: Hong Kong's busiest harbor was named Victoria Harbour in the 1850s after a fleet of ships belonging to the British monarch, Queen Victoria, docked there.

······ **Bamboo and canvas sail**

Captain

In Deep Water: Victoria Harbour has a depth of 43 m (141 ft) at its deepest point. This allows huge, heavyweight ships to move around the port.

Hong Kong Peak: The highest point on Hong Kong Island is Mount Austin, which is 1,713 ft (522m) high.

The Great Wall of China: At 13,170 miles (21,196 km) long, the Great Wall of China is the longest wall in the world. Running across the rugged mountains of northern China, some parts of this giant ancient structure are over 2,000 years old.

355—the number of skyscrapers in Hong Kong, which is more than any other city in the world.

Lightweight wood

Junk boats: These ancient Chinese sailing boats have been used for fishing and trading since the Han dynasty of China, which lasted from 206 BCE–220 CE.

7.5 million—the number of people that live in Hong Kong, making it one of the most densely populated places in the world.

TOKYO

Lying off the east coast of Asia, Japan is an island country home to one of the most crowded cities in the world: Tokyo. Shibuya Crossing is Tokyo's busiest road crossing with millions of people hurrying across its packed streets every day. It is a bustling place where people meet friends, eat, and shop.

バーゲン

靴

新しい!

東京へようこそ

Heavy Footfall: As many as 2,500 people cross Shibuya Crossing every time the traffic stops for a red light.

こちらへ

寿司

2.4 million—the number of people that pass through Shibuya Crossing every day!

止まって!

noodles

Tokyo Food Show: There are many food stalls next to Shibuya Crossing selling an exciting range of snacks, such as octopus on a stick and grilled eel.

Japanese Pagodas: Usually built as part of a Buddhist temple, pagodas are tall wooden towers with up to five levels. Each level symbolizes an element, with earth at the bottom, space at the top, and water, fire, and wind in the middle. Pagodas usually store precious items and holy relics.

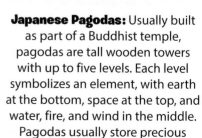

Ultra-modern: Tokyo is famous for its neon billboards, colorful advertisements, and bright lights.

People Watching: With huge, floor-to-ceiling windows, the cafés overlooking the crossing are a go-to place for people-watching.

Saying Hello: In Japan, people greet each other with a bow. The lower the bow, the more respect it shows.

Hollywood Stardom: As one of the most iconic sights in Japan, Shibuya Crossing has appeared in several famous blockbuster films.

Standing Strong: Shibuya Crossing has existed for over 100 years, since the Shibuya Station was built in 1885.

THE MARIANA TRENCH

In the Pacific Ocean, somewhere between Hawaii and the Philippines, is a giant chasm in the ocean floor called the Mariana Trench. This is the deepest place on Earth and home to all sorts of strange and wonderful deep-sea creatures that have adapted to the extreme environment.

Mountains Deep: The Mariana Trench is 36,201 ft (11,034 m) deep. That's deep enough to fit Mount Everest—the highest mountain on Earth—inside it.

.... **Dumbo octopus**

Spooky Fish: The Pacific barreleye fish has a soft, see-through head and barrel-like eyes that point upward, watching for prey.

.... **Goblin shark**

Odd Animals: With nearly freezing temperatures and constant darkness, very few living things survive here. Those that do include anglerfish, viperfish, barreleye fish, goblin sharks, and Dumbo octopuses.

1,554 miles (2,500 km)—the length of the Mariana Trench, which is more than five times the length of the Grand Canyon.

Viperfish ....

Anglerfish: This nightmarish fish lives at depths of over 6,600 ft (2,000 m). It has a glowing fin on its head that attracts fish into its gaping, toothy mouth.

Hagfish: These eel-shaped creatures live at depths of up to 5,600 ft (1,700 m) and can go for months without food. When they can, they feed on dead animals that have sunk from above, tunneling deep into the flesh. They produce a slippery slime, which they sneeze out through their nostrils.

Anglerfish . . . .

High Pressure: The pressure in the Mariana Trench is 1,000 times higher than above sea level because of the weight of water pressing down from above.

Into the Unknown: Only a handful of divers have descended into Challenger Deep, which is the very deepest place within the trench.

Australasia

Australasia is a region that includes Australia, the world's smallest continent, and a number of Pacific islands, including New Zealand. With dust-filled deserts and tropical rain forests to explore, Australasia is a land full of adventure.

Hop along with kangaroos in the remote Australian Outback, swim with multicolored fish at the world's longest barrier reef, and hike through dense rain forests in search of the secretive cassowary bird. Then, take a trip to Sydney where breathtaking fireworks light up the sky, and jet across to New Zealand to climb the towering mountains of the Southern Alps.

ANTARCTICA

South of Australasia, at the most southerly place on Earth around the South Pole, is the continent of Antarctica. The land is covered by vast shelves of ice many miles thick and few animals or plants can survive in the extreme cold. This is the only continent on which humans have never permanently lived.

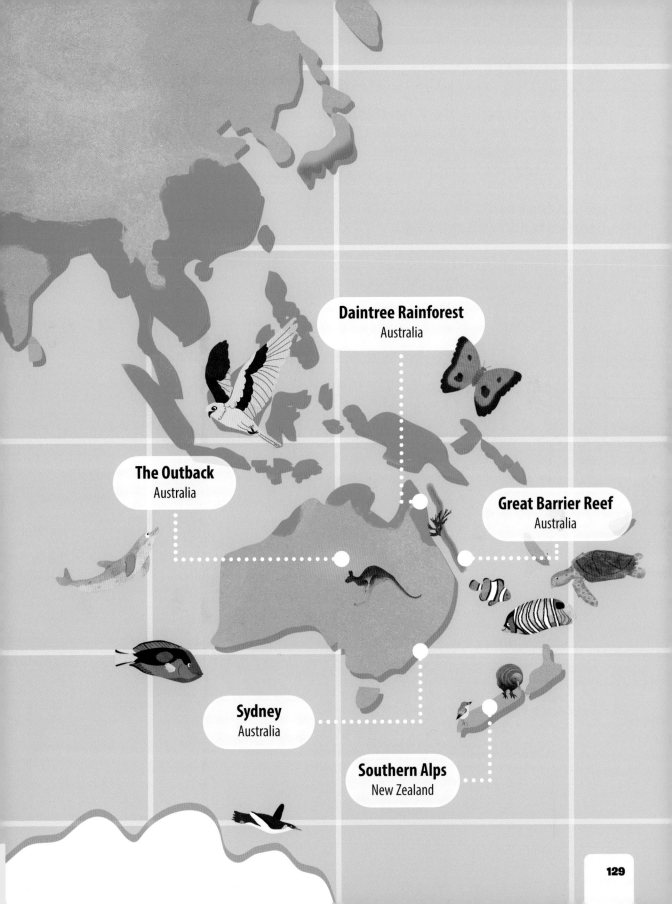

Daintree Rainforest
Australia

The Outback
Australia

Great Barrier Reef
Australia

Sydney
Australia

Southern Alps
New Zealand

SYDNEY

Sydney is the capital city of New South Wales on the east coast of Australia. The city is known for its vibrant culture, yacht-filled harbor, beaches, and iconic Harbour Bridge. Founded in 1788, the city has grown to become the largest and busiest city in Australia, drawing people from all over the world.

Sydney Harbour: With sandy beaches, walkways, and green gardens lining its shores, Sydney Harbour is a beautiful place to take a stroll.

New Year's Fireworks: Most years, Sydney holds one of the biggest annual events in the world with around 9 tons (8.2 tonnes) of fireworks lighting up the skies.

1 million—the number of spectators that gather in Sydney Harbour on New Year's Eve to watch the dazzling firework displays.

Multicultural: Of the five million people that live in Sydney, more than two million were born in other parts of the world.

Great Heights: The Sydney Harbour Bridge is around 440 ft (134 m) tall. Its exact height varies by up to 7 in (18 cm) depending on the temperature.

Sydney Opera House: On the edge of the harbor water is Sydney Opera House where people can enjoy music, opera, dance, theater and comedy. The building took 10,000 construction workers 14 years to build, and was finally completed in 1973.

Sydney Harbour is home to the oldest sailing event in the world, which has been held since 1837.

250—the number of languages spoken in Sydney, with some of the most common being English, Cantonese, Arabic, and Greek.

DAINTREE RAINFOREST

In the northeast corner of Australia, the Daintree Rainforest is a magical landscape that is bigger than the city of Sydney. With soaring mountains, tumbling waterfalls, fast-flowing streams, and extraordinary wildlife, there's plenty to explore here. The forest is millions of years older than the Amazon and home to a rare and endangered bird called the cassowary, which hides deep in the forest.

180 million years old— the age of the Daintree Rainforest, making it the oldest tropical rain forest in the world.

Giant Birds: The female cassowary bird can reach 6.5 ft (2 m) tall, which is taller than most adult humans! These prehistoric-looking birds have large bristly wings but cannot fly, and dagger-sharp claws that they use to defend their nests.

Heavy Egg: Cassowary eggs weigh around 1.3 lb (580 g) and are the third largest of all bird eggs.

···· **Cassowary chick**

Two Natural Wonders: At the northern edge of the Daintree Rainforest, the tropical trees meet white-sand beaches. Beyond the shoreline, a beautiful coral reef stretches out to sea.

Kuku Yalanji People: For over 9,000 years, Aboriginal people have lived in the rain forest. Songs, stories, and traditional skills, like spear fishing and catching crabs, have been passed down by these people for thousands of years.

3,000—the number of plant species that grow in the Daintree Rainforest, and these plants are home to at least 12,000 species of insects.

Ulysses butterfly

Saltwater Crocodiles: Along winding waterways, saltwater crocodiles lie in wait for prey. With the strongest bite of any animal, their huge jaw muscles bulge out on either side of their heads.

THE OUTBACK

The Australian Outback spans across the dry heart of Central Australia, encompassing rusty-red sand dunes, gray stone mountains, and remote desert landscapes. In the Northern Territory, the Newhaven Wildlife Sanctuary provides a safe home for many of the native and endangered species of the Outback. Australia's largest native land animal, the red kangaroo, lives here in small groups called mobs.

1,012 sq miles (2,620 sq km)— the size of the wildlife sanctuary, which is surrounded by a fence to protect the native wildlife from feral cats and foxes.

Uluru: Located in the south of the Northern Territory, Uluru is a massive sandstone rock standing 1,142 ft (348 m) high, which is taller than the Eiffel Tower in Paris. Uluru is a sacred place for the local Indigenous people who have lived in the area for 30,000 years.

The scenery at Newhaven Wildlife Sanctuary varies from copper-red sand dunes to crusty salt lakes and prickly, low-lying shrubs.

174—the number of bird species in Newhaven Wildlife Sanctuary.

Mulga tree ·······

Marsupials: Australia is home to 250 species of marsupial, including kangaroos, koalas, and wombats. After birth, a marsupial baby lives in a pouch on its mother's belly until it is strong enough to stand by itself.

······ **Wild camel**

30 ft (9m)—how far a male red kangaroo can leap in a single hop.

Wild Camping: Between April and September, visitors can camp in the sanctuary to explore hiking trails and birdwatching spots.

New-born: A baby kangaroo, or joey, is blind and hairless when it is born. At just 1 in (2.5 cm) in length, it is about the same size as a grape!

Camels: Wild camels can grow even bigger than kangaroos, but unlike native kangaroos, camels were brought to Australia in the 19th century. Today, there are more than one million feral camels living wild in Australia's deserts.

GREAT BARRIER REEF

As the world's largest coral reef system, the Great Barrier Reef is one of the natural wonders of the world. It stretches right along the coast of Queensland in Northeast Australia and is home to a variety of ocean habitats. Here, you can explore the coral reef by boat, or swim and dive alongside extraordinary wildlife.

1,400 miles (2,300 km)—the length of the Great Barrier Reef, which is bigger than the UK, Switzerland, and the Netherlands combined.

Reefs and Islands: The Great Barrier Reef is made up of 3,000 separate reefs and 900 islands.

115 ft (35 m)—the depth of water near the shoreline, but in the outer reefs, the seabed slopes down to a depth of 6,600 ft (2,000 m).

. . . Clownfish

Rainbow Colors: More than 1,500 species of colorful fish live in the Great Barrier Reef, which is 10 percent of the world's fish species. They include clownfish, blue tang, and regal angelfish.

Bottlenose dolphin

Sea Turtles: These gentle creatures can live up to 80 years and have existed since prehistoric times.

Blue tang ......

More than 30 species of dolphins and whales feed and play around the reef, including bottlenose dolphins and humpback whales.

Regal angelfish

Underwater Worlds: You can snorkel and scuba dive in many amazing habitats around the Great Barrier Reef, exploring coral reefs, sandy banks, and seagrass meadows.

Colorful Coral: There are around 600 types of coral living in the Great Barrier Reef. Corals are formed by the skeletons of tiny creatures called polyps. The bright colors are produced by algae that live within the polyps. A single polyp can begin an entire reef!

Habitat Loss: The Great Barrier Reef is under threat due to human actions and climate change. Rising sea temperatures are damaging the coral reefs, bleaching the coral (turning it white), and destroying this precious natural habitat.

SOUTHERN ALPS

Located in the southwestern Pacific Ocean, New Zealand is made up of two islands—the North Island and the South Island. The South Island is the largest and home to glistening lakes, creaking glaciers and the country's longest mountain range—the Southern Alps.

Kea ·······

Majestic Mountains: The Southern Alps are a chain of rugged, snow-capped mountains that stretch for 300 miles (500 km). Many peaks are over 9,800 ft (3,000 m) high.

Serene Lake: People come to watch native birds and fish for salmon at Lake Mapourika, which is the largest lake on the west coast of South Island.

Pukeko

Antarctica: Less than 3,100 miles (5,000 km) away from New Zealand's South Island is the ice-covered continent of Antarctica. This is the most southern place on Earth and the location of the South Pole. Antarctica is an extreme frozen environment with very few people, but emperor penguins roam wild across the ice.

New Zealand falcon

New Zealand was first settled by humans 700 years ago, when Maori people arrived from Polynesia.

12,218 ft (3,724 m)—the height of Aoraki/Mount Cook, which is the highest mountain in New Zealand.

Kea

14,000 years ago—when Lake Mapourika was formed from a giant block of ice left behind by a melting glacier.

Native Birds: The Southern Alps are a bird-watcher's paradise. The kea, a large alpine parrot, and the New Zealand falcon can be seen flying above the landscape, whereas the flightless kiwi, New Zealand's national animal, can be seen rooting around at ground level.

Nose to the Ground: Kiwis are the only birds with nostrils at the end of their beaks. They use them to sniff out food among fallen leaves.

1 in (3 cm)—the length of a kiwi's wings, which means it can't fly, although it can outrun most humans.

Glossary

ALGAE A type of plant-like living thing, such as seaweed, that grows in water.

ALTITUDE The height of a place in relation to sea level.

ANCESTOR A person who has lived previously and from whom one can be descended.

AZTEC EMPIRE An ancient civilization that existed in central Mexico between around 1300 and 1521.

BIODIVERSITY The variety of plant and animal life within a habitat.

CANOPY The very top layer of branches in a forest, where most leaves and foliage are.

CIVILISATION The people, culture, and way of life in a particular place.

COMMUNIST Part of a political movement that aims to share wealth and resources to create an "equal society."

CONSERVATION Protecting plants, animals, and habitats from the harmful effects of human activities, such as pollution.

CYCLONE A storm, or system of high winds, that rotates around a central point, also known as a hurricane.

DESERT A landscape where very little rain falls, making the environment hostile for most plants and animals.

DNA Short for deoxyribonucleic acid. Inside the cells of living things, DNA carries information about how a living thing will look and behave.

DORMANT (VOLCANO) A volcano that is not currently erupting, but is expected to erupt again.

DROUGHT A period when rain is extremely rare, creating very dry conditions and water shortages.

ENDANGERED At risk of becoming extinct, often due to habitat loss or climate change.

ENDEMIC A plant or animal that is native (an original inhabitant) in a certain place and only lives there.

EXPORT A product or service from a country that is sold abroad in other countries.

FOOD CHAIN A way of showing how plants and animals get their energy, with each living thing in the food chain relying on the next living thing for food.

FORTRESS A type of strong building that is designed to withstand attack and protect the people inside.

FOSSILIZED When the remains of a plant or animal are preserved inside rock, creating a fossil.

FRESHWATER Water that is not salty, for example, the water that makes up lakes, rivers, and streams.

GLACIER A large mass of slow-moving ice.

HABITAT The natural home of a plant or animal.

HIBERNATE When an animal spends the winter in a sleep-like state, only waking when the season changes.

ICE AGE A period of colder global temperatures, when thick ice sheets cover large parts of Earth's surface.

INDIGENOUS Living things, including people, that are the original inhabitants of a place.

INTERNATIONAL SPACE STATION A space station that orbits Earth, where astronauts live and work.

LAGOON An area of saltwater that is separated from the sea by a natural land barrier, such as a reef.

LANDLOCKED A country or region that is surrounded by other countries and has no coastline.

LIGHT POLLUTION The brightening of the night-sky caused by man-made light, such as street lamps.

LOGGING The action of cutting down trees in order to use the wood.

MAMMAL An animal that has a backbone and, when young, is nourished by milk from its mother.

MARSUPIAL A type of mammal that isn't properly developed when it is born and continues growing inside a pouch on its mother's belly.

MIGRATION The journey that an animal makes to a different place, often when the season changes.

MONARCH The person that rules over a kingdom or empire, such as a queen or emperor.

MUMMIFIED When the body of a dead human or animal is preserved and wrapped in cloth.

NECTAR The sweet liquid that is made by flowers to attract bees for pollination.

NOMADIC A person with no fixed home, who chooses to travel from place to place.

NUTRIENT Something that provides nourishment and is essential to the survival of living things.

OBSERVATORY A building that houses equipment that is used to study the stars and planets.

ORBIT The regular, repeating pattern that one object in space takes around another; for example, the Moon around the Earth or the Earth around the Sun.

PLANKTON Tiny living things that are found in water.

PLATEAU A relatively flat area of land that sits higher up than the land around it.

PREHISTORIC The period of history that is earlier than any existing human records.

PREY An animal that is hunted by another for food.

RADIO ANTENNA A device that picks up radio waves.

RAIN FOREST A forest that receives a very high level of rainfall and supports a rich variety of living things.

RELIC An object from the past that has been kept because of its historical significance.

REPTILE An animal with a backbone that has dry, scaly skin and usually lays eggs on land, such as a snake, a crocodile, or a lizard.

RODENT A type of mammal with sharp front teeth that grow throughout its life, such as a rat or a mouse.

SCANDINAVIAN Belonging to one of a group of countries in northern Europe, including Denmark, Norway, and Sweden.

SPECIES A group of animals or plants that share similar characteristics.

STATE A nation or territory that is governed as one community.

TEMPERATE A region or climate that experiences mild temperatures.

TROPICAL Relating to Earth's regions close to the Equator, where temperatures are hot and humid.

VENOMOUS When an animal is able to make poison (venom), which it can pass on through a bite or a sting.

WORLD HERITAGE SITE An important natural or man-made place that is protected for future generations of people to see.

Index

Index